Planning for Teaching

by Janet A. Wessel and Ellen Curtis-Pierce

Fearon Teacher Aids
Belmont, California

Designed and Illustrated by Rose C. Sheifer

ISBN 0-8224-5355-X

Printed in the United States of America

1. 9 8 7 6 5 4 3 2 1

Contents

Introduction **5**
Long-Term Planning 5

Planning the Unit and Lesson **11**
Introduction 11
Planning the Teaching Unit 11
Planning the Lesson 12
In Summary: Direct Instruction 17

Planning a Home Activities Program **27**
Introduction 27
The Planning Steps 27

Social Skills Planning Guide **37**
Getting Started...37
Social Skills 38
Follow Directions 39
Participate with Others 40
Respect the Rights of Others 41
Task Persistence 42
Independent Problem Solving 43
Social Skills Checklists 44

Appendices **54**
A. Planning Worksheets for Teaching 54
B. Planning Worksheets for Home Activities Program 64
C. Master List of Action Words 70
D. Master List of Games Matched to Objective 75
E. A Toy Guide for Children with Special Needs 85

Introduction

There are eight books in this Play and Motor Skills Activities Series for preschool and early primary children with special needs.

1. Locomotor Activities
2. Ball-Handling Activities
3. Stunts and Tumbling Activities
4. Health Fitness Activities
5. Rhythmic Activities
6. Body Management Activities
7. Play Activities
8. Planning for Teaching

What Is Planning for Teaching?

Planning for teaching is the decision-making process before, during, and after teaching to ensure each child's success in achieving the desired learning outcomes. Careful preparation sets the stage for effective instruction. Knowledge of children and of the skill to be taught are prerequisites to instructional excellence. But successful planning also rests on your ability to anticipate the child's needs and behaviors. Preinstructional preparation involves not only the selection of basic instructional procedures but also your creativity in planning for the experience.

Meeting the special needs of the children does not just happen during teaching. It must be planned.

What Is Covered in This Book?

Planning for Teaching is a how-to guide. Its purpose is to help you plan instruction that meets the individual needs of each child. It provides a step-by-step procedure to guide your decision making. The how-to steps are presented under three major preinstructional planning activities:

1. Planning the Unit and Lesson
2. Planning a Home Activities Program
3. Social Skills Planning Guide

Materials in the seven activity books that are used in planning are identified. Planning worksheets and master lists of games and action words are provided as appendices at the end of this book. Planning worksheets can be reproduced as needed.

LONG-TERM PLANNING

The planning process begins when you decide which skills are to be taught, why they will be taught, and when. The decision-makers establish the goals of the program, select objectives for the children to achieve those goals, sequence the objectives across the school years, and set expectations of when children will achieve mastery of the objectives. The outcome of these decisions is the Scope and Sequence Chart, a curriculum plan with explicit intended outcomes.

The Scope and Sequence Chart

This chart is the teacher's long-range plan. It clearly states the purpose and goals of teaching from the time the teaching begins. The objectives are the essential skills, the core learnings, and what the school and community wish the children to acquire and experience as they progress toward achieving the goals. Because of the nature of fitness and social skills, they are worked on continuously to help the child develop and maintain a desirable level of performance. As the child grows and matures, appropriate performance standards of the school or district can be developed according to that child's expectancies. The Scope and Sequence Chart is reviewed and evaluated each year based on the child's performance. Recommendations for changes (what and when a skill is taught) are based on the class and each child's Individual Record of Progress.

An example of a scope and sequence chart developed for a four-year play and motor skill school program for children with special needs is presented as Form 8.1 (pp. 8–9).

The teachers, the director, and the parents involved in this program reviewed the goals and objectives presented in the seven activity books. Using a consensus decision-making technique, they made their final decisions about goals, objectives, and sequences. Each person ranked the goals and objectives independently. Discussion followed. Then each person independently ranked them again. The average ratings were determined. These ratings served to rank the goals and objectives and to sequence the objectives for the four-year skills program.

Key Decision-Making Considerations

The three key points that the group considered in developing a long-term program were time, number of objectives, and sequence of objectives.

1. *Available time and time needed for meaningful gain.* The teachers decided it would take their children 200 minutes to make meaningful gain on each objective (two or more skill components) and 600 minutes to achieve functional mastery level performance. The total time available for instruction in one school year was calculated (see Appendix A, Worksheet 2 for more about time calculations):

30 minutes per day x 180 days = 5,400 minutes

minus flex or lost time   −540 minutes

Total available time = 4,860 minutes

2. *Total number of essential objectives selected for mastery.* The total number of essential objectives for mastery was determined by dividing the total number of minutes (4,860) by 600 minutes for mastery:

$$\frac{4,860}{600} = 8.1 \text{ essential objectives per year}$$

The essential objectives selected for the four-year program (total of 32) would be considered the core learnings. Teachers could add other objectives as time permitted and as their children achieved or progressed toward mastery of the essential objectives or desired outcomes.

Mastery level implies that the child has mastered the skill to a degree that that skill can be used in the home, at school, or in the neighborhood. Mastery for some children may be Skill Level 2 and for others, 1 or 3. Mastery will depend on the opportunities the child has for instruction and guided practice, the child's level of comprehension, and the complexity of the skill itself.

The initial level of the child's performance will determine the number of times (units of instruction) the child will require to progress toward mastery. For example, a 4-year-old child entering at Skill Level 2 may require instruction on this skill at ages 5 and 6 before mastery is achieved, while a child entering at Skill Level 1 may require more intensive instruction during the school years, such as a Home Activities Program matched to the teaching units during the school year.

3. *Goal emphasis across the four years.* The final planning decision was to select the essential objectives and then sequence them to emphasize each goal area. Some goals (such as body management skills) were considered more important than others in the early years. The goals of social and fitness skills were constant across all years. The number of objectives per goal area in the Scope and Sequence Chart (Form 8.1)

indicates the emphasis the teachers placed on each goal area.

Social Skills

Planning for social skills began when the teachers decided that helping the child to grow and develop socially in learning and playing with others was an important goal and should be included in the Scope and Sequence Chart. Next, they identified specific social skills and behaviors that were considered the most important for the child with special needs to exhibit in order to succeed in learning and playing with others in integrated activities.

The following social skills and behaviors were identified by the teachers, using consensus decision making:

1. *Respect the rights of others:* take turns, share equipment, ask permission to borrow, care for and use the equipment purposefully, and help others.
2. *Participate with others:* watch and listen to others, invite others to play, choose to join others in play, assume a role in playing, and work with others toward a common goal.
3. *Task persistence:* attempt a task, ask for help, try again, complete a task, and do not disrupt others.
4. *Follow directions:* nonverbal and verbal directions, one-part directions, two-part directions, and a set of directions.
5. *Independent problem solving:* make a choice to work independently on assigned task, try different ways to solve the problem, seek assistance when needed, evaluate success, and use the skill in similar activities.

With identification of the social skill and specific behaviors to be exhibited by the child, the teachers developed a Social Skills Planning Guide. The purpose of the guide was to help teachers plan for teaching of the skills.

The planning guide along with individual checklists and records of progress developed by the teachers for these social skills is

presented on pages 37–53. You may decide to use these social skills or to adapt them or develop new ones to meet the children's needs in planning units and lessons.

How Much Planning?

Few teachers and administrators deny the importance of and necessity for planning. Some feel that the Scope and Sequence Chart with lesson planning is enough. Others stress the importance of the Scope and Sequence Chart and the yearly program plan and minimize lesson planning.

The yearly program plan encompasses sequential unit plans over the school year. A unit plan consists of the objectives and time allocations for each objective based on the Scope and Sequence Chart. Compatible objectives are grouped together for teaching and are sequenced across the year.

Planning needs of teachers, as well as school requirements, also vary. Whether a Scope and Sequence Chart and a yearly program of sequential units derived from the chart are developed depends most often on the administration's requirement. To meet the special needs of children and to ensure each child's success in achieving the desired learning outcomes, however, the teaching unit and lesson plan based on the unit plan are important. Together, the teaching unit and lesson plan make up the overall teaching plan.

FORM 8.1
THE SCOPE AND SEQUENCE CHART: THE LONG-TERM PROGRAM PLAN

Key: X = Skills are introduced and taught.

M = Mastery level expectations (teacher adapts level of mastery in response to child's needs). Children may master many of these skills earlier than reflected on this chart.

Goals and Objectives Assessed	Age Range				Skills Added or Deleted Based on Priority Rankings and Needs of Children
	3–4	4–5	5–6	6–7	
1. Locomotor and Rhythmic Skills					
Climb	X	X	X	M	
Run	X	X	X	M	
Hop		X	X	M	
Jump	X	X	X	M	
Gallop	X	X	M		
Skip		X	X	M	
Slide			X	X	
Even Beat	X	X	M		
Uneven Beat		X	X	M	
Accent		X	X	M	
Expressive Movement	M				
Singing Games	X	X	X	X	
2. Ball-Handling Skills					
Bounce a Ball		X	X	M	
Catch a Ball	X	X	X	M	
Hit a Ball	X	X	X	M	
Kick a Ball	X	X	M		
Roll a Ball	X	X	M		
Throw a Ball (underhand)	X	X	M		
3. Health and Physical Fitness Skills (mastery level commensurate with age and capacity)					
Walk-Run	X	X	X	X	
Situps	X	X	X	X	
Trunk-Leg Flexibility	X	X	X	X	
Rest and Relaxation	X	X	X	X	
Lift and Carry Objects	X	X	X	X	

FORM 8.1 (CONTINUED)

Goals and Objectives Assessed	Age Range				Skills Added or Deleted Based on Priority Rankings and Needs of Children
	3–4	4–5	5–6	6–7	
4. Body Management Skills (including Stunts and Tumbling)					
Body Actions	X	M			
Body Parts	X	X	M		
Directions in Space	X	X	M		
Use of Space	X	X	M		
Shapes and Sizes		X	X	M	
Log Roll	X	M			
Forward Roll	X	X	M		
Backward Roll		X	X	M	
Static Balance	X	M			
Dynamic Balance	X	X	X	M	
Parachute		X	X	M	
5. Play Skills					
Push and Pull Object	X	M			
Travel on a Scooterboard		X	X	M	
Hang from a Bar		X	X	M	
Ride Tricycle or Bicycle		X	X	M	
Slide Down a Slide	X	X	M		
Swing on a Swing	X	M			
6. Social Skills (mastery level commensurate with age and capacity)					
Follow Directions	X	X	X	X	
Participate with Others	X	X	X	X	
Respect Rights of Others	X	X	X	X	
Task Persistence	X	X	X	X	
Independent Problem Solving	X	X	X	X	

Planning the Unit and Lesson

INTRODUCTION

A teaching unit is a group of compatible instructional objectives that are sequenced over a period of teaching time. Instructional and evaluation activities are derived and lessons are planned from this unit.

A teaching unit plan normally ranges from three to six weeks. It consists of sequential unit lesson plans, the objectives, the time allocated, and the selection of play and game activities. Teachers may decide to develop a yearly unit plan or begin with one or two units.

Lesson plans evolve from the unit plan. They are an expanded portion of the unit plan. The lesson plans may extend beyond a single class period. They contain the objectives, the time allocations for teaching each objective, the groups of children based on performance or diagnostic testing, and the play and game activities prescribed to help each child achieve success.

Why Is Planning Important?

Preinstructional planning is essential. The teaching unit is a road map, a plan of action. Teachers must plan the children's experiences. They must plan the scope and sequence of the yearly program: the units to be taught, the activities to be employed, and the performance or diagnostic tests to be given.

The unit plan is fundamental to planning lessons designed to meet each child's needs. It provides a structure around which specific individual and class activities are organized. It provides a structure for making adjustments to help each child achieve the desired learning outcomes.

Adjustments in the unit and lesson plans are to be expected. The adjustments are based on the experiences and performances of the children during instruction. They are noted on the unit and lesson plans and can be recycled to improve instruction.

PLANNING THE TEACHING UNIT

The planning steps and the resources available in the seven activity books are identified in the box below:

PLANNING THE TEACHING UNIT

How Is It Done?

1. Select compatible objectives to be taught in the four-week unit (e.g., objectives that use the same equipment, that are all for indoor or for outdoor facilities, or that are for the same season). Avoid skills that have similar skill components, such as over- and underhand throws, that may cause learning problems for some children.
2. Develop unit lesson plans by sequencing objectives across the unit with time allocated for teaching each objective.
3. Develop play and game activity plans for the unit.

Resource: Activity Books

Objectives (eight per year) in the Scope and Sequence Chart or Yearly Program Plan, if developed

Game lesson plan sheets in each activity book or master game sheet in *Planning for Teaching*

THE TEACHING UNIT

Some teachers develop units for a yearly program plan. Others develop the teaching units one at a time. No matter what approach you take, however, the steps and unit format are the same.

An example of a teaching unit is shown in Form 8.2 (p. 13). The unit objectives were selected from the eight essential objectives identified in the Scope and Sequence Chart. In this sample unit, four essential objectives were selected: Catching a Ball, two fitness objectives (Situps and Walk-Run), and one social skill objective (Follow Directions).

The time allocated for each objective is determined by the time available during the unit and by the total time needed for the child to make meaningful gain in the one or two skill components of that objective. The fitness objectives and the social skill objectives are taught throughout all units during the year. The time allocated for the Catching a Ball objective is based on the time the teachers determined would be needed for meaningful gain (200 minutes per skill objective).

The Unit Games and Play Activity Plan

Teachers find that developing unit games and play activity plans helps them compile a list of instructional activities geared to teaching specific performance objectives and skills during the year. Once completed, these lists provide concise information on prescribed activities. This is not only valuable for the teacher, but it also informs substitute teachers and the principal about what is to be taught. A unit games and play activity plan for the Catching a Ball objective is shown in Form 8.3 (p. 14). The games listed in the example were selected from the activity books.

The lists eliminate the need to search for activities. They can be used as a record. You can delete those activities that do not work, add others, and adapt the activities. These changes can be written on the planning activity sheet for the unit. At the end of the year, a complete record of what worked, what did not work, or what needed to be adapted is available for future teaching and planning.

PLANNING THE LESSON

The planning steps and the resources available in the seven activity books are identified in the box "Planning the Lesson."

PLANNING THE LESSON: INDIVIDUALIZING INSTRUCTION

How Is It Done?	Resource: Activity Books*
1. Performance or diagnostic testing (unit objectives)	Checklists: Class and Individual Records of Progress; Learning Centers
2. Designing a lesson plan	Getting Started, Performance Objectives (skill components), Teaching Activities, Action Words, Game Sheet Lesson Plans, Learning Centers
3. Evaluating child's progress and effectiveness of instruction	Checklists: Class and Individual Records of Progress; Unit and Yearly Reports

* Social skills performance objectives and checklists are found in the Social Skills Planning Guide in this book.

FORM 8.2
TEACHING UNIT LESSON PLAN

Projected Timeline:

_____ to _____

Teacher: _____

Gym Days/Times: _____

Objectives:

_____

_____

School: _____

Level: _____

Continue Schedule
Recording Child's Perform-
ance on Class Record of
Progress

200 minutes total on Catching a Ball, divided into 20 minutes daily instruction = 10 days/3 days per week = 3 weeks and 1 day teaching unit. Fitness objectives taught periodically throughout all units. Social skills are taught similarly and become part of class management procedures.

FORM 8.3
UNIT GAMES AND PLAY ACTIVITY PLAN

Unit No.: _____   Level: _____   Objective: _____

ACTIVITY	ORGANIZATION	DESCRIPTION/INSTRUCTIONS	EQUIPMENT

Performance or Diagnostic Testing

To individualize your lesson plans, you need to know what the child can do and what the child needs to achieve. Use the performance objectives (skills) you've selected for the unit to assess the child's skills. The objectives align the curriculum with testing and evaluating as shown in "The Story of Performance or Diagnostic Testing" (p. 16).

Performance or diagnostic testing is conducted before instruction on the objective to be taught. Knowing the performance criteria (skill components and levels), you can set up an activity and observe the child's performance. To observe and assess a child, you should follow these steps:

1. Get the child's attention.
2. Demonstrate and ask the child to perform the skill.
3. Give a practice trial.
4. If necessary, provide additional demonstration, verbal request, and practice trial where there are no distractions.
5. The child performs the skill the required number of times.
6. Reinforce the child throughout.
7. Record the assessment results.

You can use the Class Record of Progress to record each child's performance. For example, performance data recorded for a class on the objective Catching a Ball is shown in Form 8.4 (p. 19).

The Lesson Plan

With your knowledge of the child's entry level of performance and ability to understand and respond to instructional cues (action words or physical prompts), you can set annual goals and short-term objectives (skill components to be achieved in a specified unit of time). Prescribing activities for a child's instructional plan in a class is the next step.

Prescribing activities involves decisions about action words, game and play activities, grouping of the children, equipment needed, arrangement of space, and rules and procedures for management of the class. To make these decisions, you need to consider the following points:

how close the child is to achieving the skill components of the objectives,

how much time is allotted in the unit for the objective,

difficulty of the objectives,

ability of the child to understand,

level of assistance required—physical prompts and assistance,

staffing available—volunteers, tutors, aides, and

type of play or game activity involvement.

Group the children for instruction on the basis of each child's assigned learning task and each child's ability to work with a partner or in a small group or large group. Children may be assigned to a small group working on the same learning tasks, or children working on different learning tasks may work as a team. Each member of the team must achieve the tasks assigned. Members can help each other. After the tasks are completed, awards can then be given to the team.

Equipment needs to be available to keep each child actively engaged in the learning task. The learning area should be arranged to ensure your children's health and safety, and the children should be able to move easily from one learning center to another. Each book provides examples of learning centers. You can easily adapt these centers to meet the needs of the children in the class and to allow for use of the equipment.

A lesson plan may run for one day or for several days. Each lesson plan consists of an introductory activity, the body, and a summary. Each activity is allotted an amount of time that is derived from the unit lesson plans. An example of a lesson plan based on the children's performance data is presented in Form 8.5 (p. 20).

THE STORY OF PERFORMANCE OR DIAGNOSTIC TESTING

The teacher has a unit plan of what the children should learn in motor and play skills during the year.

Program Goals
1. Ball-Handling Skills
   a. Catching a Ball
   b. Rolling a Ball

The teacher selects and develops performance-objective criteria to find out how well each student can demonstrate the skill components of the different skills.

From the test results, the teacher can tell which skills each child has and has not learned.

With this information, the teacher can plan each child's individual learning program, assign learning tasks (skill component and skill level), set expectations, and prescribe instructional activities.

Sam is placed in a group of students who will practice hand control of the ball.

Carl is placed in a group of students who will learn to use their arms to absorb the force of the ball.

Mary is placed in a group of students who will learn to improve the preparatory phase and eye focus.

You can record day-by-day adjustments on the lesson plan. Then note the changes on the unit lesson plans. These changes will help you keep a record of what works and what does not work in teaching the objective. Use these notes to plan for teaching the next time around or for the next unit.

Evaluating and Reporting

Monitoring a child's progress during instruction is essential to individualized instruction. As the child's performance changes, note it on the Record of Progress. You can adjust the prescription to meet the child's needs during instruction. As soon as you observe success or nonsuccess, adjust the child's instructional plan. The objective may be too easy or too difficult, or a different grouping or a game or play activity of more interest may be needed.

Monitoring and assessing varies from teacher to teacher. Some teachers like to do pre- and postassessments of the children. Other teachers set times for pre-, middle, and postassessments. Still others prefer continuous assessment while teaching a unit. What is essential, however, is preassessing the children on objectives to be taught. Without these data, you won't be able to individualize the lesson plans.

The purpose of evaluation is to measure a child's progress and determine the effectiveness of instruction. By counting the skill components the child has achieved and recording the total number, you have a record of the child's progress. The Record of Progress for the class documents a particular child's progress. The reassessment data for the Catching a Ball objective is shown in Form 8.6 (p. 21).

You should review each child's record and evaluate it for success, or meaningful gain. If the expected gains for the child are achieved, you can decide to move to the next objective, to identify other skill components, or to move to the next skill level. If the progress is not acceptable, you have several planning

options: terminate instruction on the objective at this time; continue instruction if the objective is of high priority, revising the prescription and planning a home activities program; or modify expectations or goals.

If the expected gain is achieved in less than the projected time, your planning options include discontinuing instruction on the objective and going to the next one; adding another objective from the priority list; or setting a higher level of expectations and continuing work on the objective (skill components or skill level).

You will prepare a unit report of the child's progress. The report can be provided to parents and can also serve as a cumulative record of the child's progress in the program. An example of a unit report developed by a group of teachers is presented in Form 8.7 (pp. 22–25).

By compiling the unit reports, the teacher has a yearly report for the child. The Unit Reports can be used as the child's Individual Education Program (IEP) Report.

IN SUMMARY: DIRECT INSTRUCTION

Individualized instruction does not just happen. It must be planned. The teaching plan (unit and lesson plans) is essential. Preplanning by all teachers ensures the success of each child in the program.

Through planning, teachers can find a workable teaching plan within the limitations of time, resources, and facilities to make the program work for children with special needs. The instruction is only as good as the results it produces for each child. The teaching plan recommended is based on direct instruction as shown in the flow chart "Direct Instruction: Teaching Plan" (p. 18).

DIRECT INSTRUCTION: TEACHING PLAN

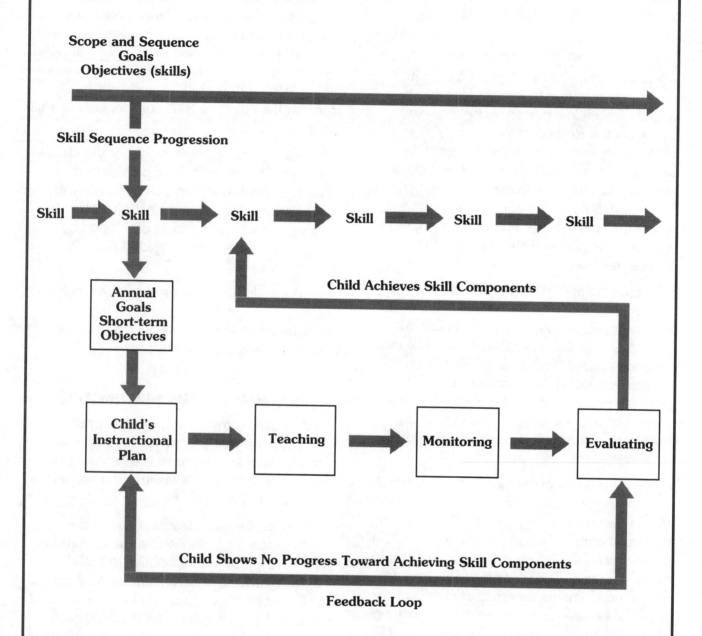

Scope and Sequence
Goals
Objectives (skills)

Skill Sequence Progression

Skill → Skill → Skill → Skill → Skill → Skill →

Child Achieves Skill Components

Annual Goals Short-term Objectives

Child's Instructional Plan → **Teaching** → **Monitoring** → **Evaluating**

Child Shows No Progress Toward Achieving Skill Components

Feedback Loop

FORM 8.4
CLASS RECORD OF PROGRESS: ASSESSMENT DATA

CLASS _____   DATE _____

AGE/GRADE _____   TEACHER _____

SCHOOL _____

OBJECTIVE: CATCHING A BALL

SCORING:	SKILL LEVEL 1		SKILL LEVEL 2				SKILL LEVEL 3	PRIMARY RESPONSES:
ASSESSMENT: _____Date **X** = Achieved **O** = Not Achieved / = Partially Achieved REASSESSMENT: _____Date ⊗ = Achieved Ø = Not Achieved	Focuses eyes on ball.	Stops ball with hands or hands and arms.	Focuses eyes on ball.	Extends arms in preparation to catch ball, elbows at sides.	Contacts and controls ball with hands or hands and arms after one bounce.	Bends elbows to absorb force of ball.	Two or more play or game activities at home or school demonstrating skill components over six-week period.	N = Not Attending NR = No Response UR = Unrelated Response O = Other (Specify in comments)
NAME	1	2	3	4	5	6	7	COMMENTS
1.								
2.								
3.								
4.								
5.								
6.								
7.								
8.								
9.								
10.								

Meaningful Gain Expectations
One or more skill components for each child in the class

_____

_____

_____

_____

_____

FORM 8.5
LESSON PLAN

Unit Plan _____ Date _____ Class _____ Time _____

Equipment _____

PHASE	ACTIVITY	TIME
Introductory Activity		
Lesson Body		
Summary		

* Numbers indicate skill component the child is to work on, based on initial assessment data shown in the Class Record of Progress

FORM 8.6
CLASS RECORD OF PROGRESS: REASSESSMENT DATA

CLASS _____   DATE _____

AGE/GRADE _____   TEACHER _____

SCHOOL _____

OBJECTIVE: CATCHING A BALL

SCORING: ASSESSMENT: _____Date X = Achieved O = Not Achieved / = Partially Achieved REASSESSMENT: _____Date ⊗ = Achieved ∅ = Not Achieved	SKILL LEVEL 1		SKILL LEVEL 2				SKILL LEVEL 3	Total skills achieved	Change plus or minus	PRIMARY RESPONSES: N = Not Attending NR = No Response UR = Unrelated Response O = Other (Specify in comments)
	Focuses eyes on ball.	Stops ball with hands or hands and arms.	Focuses eyes on ball.	Extends arms in preparation to catch ball, elbows at sides.	Contacts and controls ball with hands or hands and arms after one bounce.	Bends elbows to absorb force of ball.	Two or more play or game activities at home or school demonstrating skill components over six-week period.			
NAME	1	2	3	4	5	6	7			COMMENTS
1.										
2.										
3.										
4.										
5.										
6.										
7.										
8.										
9.										
10.										

Meaningful Gain Expectations
One or more skill components for each child in the class

_____

_____

_____

_____

_____

Unit and Yearly Report

CHILD: _____

	Marking Period	Date
LEVEL: _____	Fall Conference (white)	from ___ to ___
YEAR: _____	Winter Conference (yellow)	from ___ to ___
TEACHER: _____	Spring Conference (pink)	from ___ to ___
SCHOOL: _____	End-of-Year (cumulative) Report (blue)	from ___ to ___

Preprimary Play and Motor Skills Activity Program

The Individual Record of Progress lists all of the objectives in which your child receives instruction during the play and motor skills program. The information reported on your child's Individual Record of Progress shows your child's entry performance and progress for a marking period. The end-of-the-year report represents your child's Individual Education Program (IEP) for the objectives selected and taught during the year.

Each objective is broken into small, measurable steps or skill components. This assists the teacher to assess what your child already knew before teaching began and to determine which step to start teaching first. One of the following symbols is marked by each step or skill component of the objective:

X = The child already knew how to perform this step before teaching it began.

O = The child did not know how to perform this step before teaching it began or after instruction of it ended.

⊗ = The child did not know how to perform this step before teaching it began, but did learn how to do it during the instruction period.

This information should be helpful to you in planning home activities to strengthen your child's play and motor skills.

Comments

_____

_____

_____

_____

_____

_____

_____

_____

INDIVIDUAL RECORD OF PROGRESS: UNIT AND YEARLY REPORT (EIGHT ESSENTIAL OBJECTIVES)

SITUPS (ABDOMINAL STRENGTH)

Date: _____

Initiates a bent-leg situp:

____ Takes a starting position (lying on back, knees bent 90 degrees, feet flat on mat, arms at sides, feet supported).

____ Curls up by tucking chin and lifting shoulders (upper back) off the mat.

____ Returns to starting position in controlled movement by uncurling and lowering head to mat.

Performs a modified situp:

____ Takes a starting position.

____ Curls up by tucking chin and lifting trunk, completes curl by touching knees with hands.

____ Returns in controlled manner by uncurling trunk and lowering head to mat, hands on thighs.

____ Does 10 or more repetitions (or meets standards appropriate for child).

____ Demonstrates above skills in two or more play or game activities at home or school.

CATCHING A BALL

Date: _____

Traps or catches rolled ball:

____ Focuses eyes on ball.

____ Stops ball with hands or hands and arms.

Catches a bounced ball:

____ Focuses eyes on ball.

____ Extends arms in preparation to catch ball, elbows at sides.

____ Contacts and controls ball with hands or hands and arms after one bounce.

____ Bends elbows to absorb force of ball.

____ Demonstrates skill in one or more play or game activities at home or school.

ROLLING A BALL

Date: _____

Rolls or pushes a ball, sitting on floor:

____ Grasps ball with one or both hands and releases in forward direction.

____ Rolls or pushes ball so that it travels at least arm's length or more.

Rolls or pushes a ball to a target:

____ Focuses eyes on target.

____ Rolls or pushes ball so that it travels at least 5 feet.

____ Rolls or pushes ball so that it travels at least 10 feet.

____ Demonstrates above skills in two or more play or game activities at home or school.

INDIVIDUAL RECORD OF PROGRESS: UNIT AND YEARLY REPORT (EIGHT ESSENTIAL OBJECTIVES)

WALK-RUN FOR ENDURANCE

Date: _____

Walk-runs continuously in any manner at moderate to fast pace for:

____ One minute.

____ Three minutes.

Walk-runs on a marked course:

____ Two minutes (with at least one period of nonsupport every ten steps).

____ Four minutes (with at least one period of nonsupport every ten steps).

____ Demonstrates above skills in two or more play or game activities at home or school.

LOG ROLL

Date: _____

Initiates a half roll:

____ Rolls from front to back, keeping arms extended overhead and legs together.

____ Rolls from back to front, keeping arms extended overhead and legs together.

Initiates a log roll:

____ Rolls from front to back, keeping arms extended overhead and legs together.

____ Rolls from back to front, keeping arms extended overhead and legs together.

____ Demonstrates above skills in two or more play or game activities at home or school.

KICKING A BALL

Date: _____

Kicks a stationary ball:

____ Focuses eyes on ball.

____ Swings lower leg forward to contact ball with foot.

____ Kicks ball so that it travels 6 feet forward.

Kicks a rolling ball:

____ Steps forward with nonkicking foot, *eyes* focused on rolling ball.

____ Swings lower leg backward in preparation for the kick.

____ Swings leg forward, contacts ball with foot, kicks ball so that it travels 8 feet.

____ Demonstrates above skill in two or more play or game activities at home or school.

INDIVIDUAL RECORD OF PROGRESS: UNIT AND YEARLY REPORT (EIGHT ESSENTIAL OBJECTIVES)

RIDE A TRICYCLE OR BICYCLE

Date: _____

Pedals a tricycle or bicycle with training wheels:

____ Assumes ready position by sitting on bike and grasping handlebars, with feet maintaining contact on pedals, and is pushed 10 feet or more.

____ Assumes ready position by sitting on bike and grasping handlebars, with feet maintaining contact on pedals, and pushes down with right foot on up pedal, pushes down with left foot on up pedal, riding 10 feet or more.

____ Assumes ready position by sitting on bike and grasping handlebars, with feet pedals in up position, pushes down with right foot, then pushes down with left foot, riding a distance of 20 feet or more.

____ Assumes ready position by sitting on bike and grasping handlebars, with feet on pedals, and rides the bike around three obstacles aligned 10 feet apart without bumping obstacles.

____ Demonstrates above skills in two or more play or game activities at home or school.

RUNNING

Date: _____

Runs a distance of 30 feet:

____ Three or more periods of nonsupport (both feet alternately off ground).

____ Arms move in opposition to legs, elbows bent.

____ Foot placed near or on line.

Runs a distance of 30 feet:

____ Five or more periods of nonsupport (both feet off ground).

____ Heel-toe placement (moderate speed), not flatfooted.

____ Swings leg, bent at 90 degrees.

____ Demonstrates above skills in two or more play or game activities at home or school.

Planning a Home Activities Program

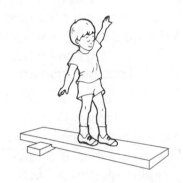

INTRODUCTION

What Is a Home Activities Program (HAP)?

HAP is an activity plan for the child carried out in the home and neighborhood. The activity plan is matched to the child's performance on the objectives taught in the teaching unit and the child's learning tasks. HAP is co-planned with the teacher and parent and, when possible, with the child.

HAP is a planned and structured activity program carried out in the home at the same time as the instructional programs and the reporting periods of the unit of instruction in school. Parents, siblings, or significant others in day care centers, hospitals, and Headstart or community recreational programs can be the home activity teacher.

Why Is It Important?

Why does a child need HAP? Because many children need a "headstart" in learning to move and moving to learn in an early childhood play and motor skill activity program. And they also need more intensive learning experiences in order to succeed in achieving desired outcomes.

These children need more time to learn, to practice, and to have guided instruction, immediate feedback, and reinforcement. The opportunity to use the skills in different settings and with different people helps these children make generalizations and retain the skill.

THE PLANNING STEPS

Step 1: Designing the Letter and the Parent Questionnaire

Prepare a letter and questionnaire for all parents to complete with you at your first meeting. The letter and questionnaire can be sent to the parents or presented at a PTA meeting. The information from the questionnaire is used to help everyone plan the HAP to fit the child's needs and interests. An example of the letter (p. 30) and of the questionnaire for parents (Form 8.8, p. 31) are shown here.

The performance objectives in the questionnaire were selected from the activities books. They are considered the most essential objectives for the children to experience and to acquire skills in during the year-long instructional program. Some teachers construct the questionnaire using the objectives for a teaching unit rather than a year's program plan.

Step 2: The Parent-Teacher Planning Meeting

The next step is to call and set a time to meet with the parent(s) in the home. During the call, explain the purpose of HAP and why it is important for the child. By meeting with the parent(s) in the home, you can gather firsthand information on the child and what the parent(s) perceive the child's needs and interests to be. If this meeting is not feasible, invite the parent(s) to the school.

The two major purposes of this meeting are (1) to explain the role of the parent(s) or others in HAP, and (2) after the decision is made to implement HAP, to set up a time for the next meeting to co-plan with the parent(s)—and the child when possible. The meeting can be held in the home or at school. Together, you and the parent(s) make this choice.

Whether or not the parent(s) decide to implement HAP, interview them and complete the questionnaire. This information is a valuable aid in helping you plan meaningful activities for the child. Also the parent(s) can gain understanding of what the instructional program is all about—the goals and objectives and the learning outcomes for the child. An interview form to obtain home information is shown in Form 8.9 (p. 32).

Step 3: Preparing for Implementation

For this step, you need to complete three activities:

1. *The child's performance record and skill illustration sheet.* From the activity books, pull the child's Individual Record of Progress for the HAP's performance objective(s). The child's entry performance is indicated on the checklist. You can easily adapt the form if you prefer a different format for the parent(s). An adapted form is shown in Form 8.10 (p. 33).

2. *Home activities log.* Time spent practicing the skill at home can be recorded in a home activities log. An example is shown in Form 8.11 (p. 34). You can adapt the form for the parent(s).

3. *Action words and games.* Decide which are the most important action words and games for the skills. Pull them from the activity books for the performance objective (skill) in HAP. To help you, there are master lists of action words and games at the end of this book. These two master lists include all the action words and games found in the activity

books for each performance objective (skill).

List the action words in the log along with the name of the game. You can reproduce the game description from the appropriate activity book and put it on the back of the log for the parent(s). If at all possible, the activities used during the HAP should be the same ones taught in classroom instruction.

At the meeting with the parent(s), present the action words, games, and the log. Make any changes at this time that are necessary to make the HAP successful for the child and the parent(s).

You may reproduce the planning worksheets in this book as needed.

Step 4: Implementing the Home Activities Program Plan

To begin implementing the program, meet with the parent(s) and the child, when possible, at home or at school. At the meeting you will

present the child's performance record and skill illustration;

demonstrate the skill components of the performance objective and what the child needs to work on (e.g., have the child perform the skill and show the parent(s) how to observe the child's movements);

present and explain the purpose of the home activity log;

discuss the action words and why they are important as verbal cues for the child's understanding and vocabulary;

explain and demonstrate the games and make changes as needed; and

explain and demonstrate assistance levels: physical assists (total or by pointing or gesturing or providing partial support during the movement; verbal cues and demonstrations for child to model; verbal cues alone) and set up of the necessary equipment to see if child will initiate the skill.

Answer all the concerns of the parent(s), then discuss location for the activities, including such points as the area in the home or yard for the activities;

the usefulness of removing extraneous noise or objects that might distract the child during the activity;

the time of day for the activities that are best for parent(s) and child, and the need for a regular routine;

the need to keep the activity sessions short (3 to 5 minutes, unless the child shows willingness and interest in continuing); and

the importance of bringing siblings or peers into the session when the child is ready to play with others.

Emphasize throughout the meeting that the goal is for the child to acquire play and motor skills in order to participate in active play activities with others at home, at school, and in the neighborhood. Most important of all, the sessions should be joyful and fun; there is no failure. To build in success, make each task smaller, provide immediate feedback and reinforcement for each trial, and find out what turns the child on: praise, hugs, pats, or playing with different equipment or people.

Next, set up a date to review and evaluate the plan. Provide a phone number for the parent(s) to call you if they need further directions.

Both you and the parent(s) can decide the schedule for reviewing and evaluating the plan. HAP can continue for several weeks or more, depending on the progress of the child. You and the parent(s) should refer to the child's Record of Progress in order to decide when to review and evaluate the program together. Or you may want to review at the end of the teaching unit.

Step 5: Evaluating the Home Activities Program Plan

The child's progress is the basis for reviewing and evaluating the merits of the HAP and for future planning.

Discuss the following questions with the parent(s). Did the child make meaningful gain toward achieving one or more skill components or skill levels of the performance objective selected for the HAP? Were the activities effective? Were the activities implemented as intended (as indicated by information provided on the home activities log)?

Once the child's progress has been evaluated and the home activities log reviewed, decide with the parent(s) what action to take. You have the following options:

If the child has made meaningful gain, continue the program on the same objective and set another meaningful gain, or stop the program on the present objective and select another one.

If the child did not make meaningful gain, continue the program with no change (more time is the crucial factor), or continue the program on the same objective and change activities (games, action words, persons, time).

If you decide to change one or more aspects of HAP, discuss these questions:

Was the skill too difficult for the child? Can it be broken down into smaller skill components?

Were expectations too high for meaningful gain?

Is there a need to increase physical and verbal prompts or to change these cues?

Is more reinforcement or simpler directions and games needed?

In addition, review the forms used by the parent(s). Do they need to be changed? Were they implemented as intended? Will visits to the home during the activities be feasible?

Some teachers set up a training program in the classroom for parents. These teachers provide the parents with a child's record and skill illustration along with selected activities. The parents serve as tutors under the supervision and monitoring of the teacher. When they are ready to implement the HAP, a meeting is scheduled. The planning steps are then implemented.

A parent self-monitor form, which was designed by a teacher and parents, helps the parent(s) implement the HAP as intended. As the example (Form 8.12, p. 35) shows, it is simply a checklist for parents.

Dear Parent,

The enclosed questionnaire has been designed to help us plan together an individualized program for your child in preprimary motor and play skills. I am interested in the kinds of play activities in which your child now participates with family, friends, and neighbors, as well as the motor and play skills you perceive that your child needs. With this information we can plan a school program for your child.

I have also enclosed a list of the year's objectives for the school program. Please check which ones you think your child already has skill in performing, those your child needs more skill in, and those that are new and that you think should be part of the program for your child.

Thank you for your help. I will call you next week to set up a time that is convenient for us to meet together as we plan this year's program for your child. If you have any questions at this time about this questionnaire, we can discuss them.

Sincerely,

(Teacher)

Form 8.8
Parent Questionnaire: The Instructional Plan

Please check (√) for your child in the appropriate column opposite each performance objective selected for the yearly program plan.

Year _____

Date _____

Essential Performance Objectives (Skills) Planned	Can Do	Needs More Help to Do Well	Needs to Learn to Do
1.			
2.			
3.			
4.			
5.			
6.			
7.			
8.			
9.			
10.			

Comments: Please list other play and motor skills you wish your child to learn. _____

_____

_____

_____

FORM 8.9
INTERVIEW FORM: HOME INFORMATION SHEET

CHILD'S NAME _____   AGE _____

RELATIONSHIP TO CHILD _____   INTERVIEW DATE _____

Interviewer: Complete the parent questionnaire (sent with letter). Then begin with these questions:

1. WHO IS THE PRIMARY CARE-GIVER FOR YOUR CHILD?
   a. Mother   d. Brother
   b. Father   e. Sister
   c. Babysitter   f. Other _____

2. HOW MUCH TIME DOES PRIMARY CARE-GIVER HAVE TO PLAY WITH YOUR CHILD EACH DAY?
   a. 15 minutes   c. 60 minutes
   b. 30 minutes   d. Other _____

3. WOULD YOU BE WILLING TO PARTICIPATE IN A HOME MOTOR SKILLS AND PLAY ACTIVITY PROGRAM FOR YOU AND YOUR CHILD?
   Yes _____   No _____

4. IF NO, WHY NOT? _____
   _____

5. IF YES, WHEN DO YOU WISH TO BEGIN? DATE: _____

6. HOW MUCH TIME WOULD YOU BE WILLING TO DEVOTE TO IT AS YOU BEGIN?
   Days per week (no.) _____   Minutes per day _____

PLAY AND GAME ACTIVITIES: HOME, NEIGHBORHOOD

What game and play activities does your child now participate in, with whom, and where? What would you like your child to be able to do in the future? (Focus on performance objectives taught in instruction.)

ACTIVITIES NOW	WITH WHOM?	WHERE?	FUTURE ACTIVITIES

FORM 8.10
INDIVIDUAL CHECKLIST AND SCORING SHEET FOR PARENT

NAME OF CHILD: _____   ACTIVITY: _____

DATE OF INITIAL PERFORMANCE: _____

Skill Illustration   Skill Components: _____

                                                _____

                                                _____

                                                _____

          [ART 8 ABOUT HERE.]   _____

                                                _____

                                                _____

                                                _____

Equipment:

_____

Directions:

_____

_____

_____

Assess the child once a week for _____ weeks, and record child's performance below.

Dates Observed	Level 1		Level 2				Level 3
	1	2	3	4	5	6	Demonstrates skill pattern in two or more activies.
Entry _____ Child's Performance							

Form 8.11
Weekly Home Activities Log Plan

Name _____ Teacher _____ Phone _____

Performance Objective _____ Date Given _____ Date Received _____

Weekly Plan _____

Parent Name _____ Parent Phone _____

Week	Dates	Times a Day	Minutes	Alone	Other Children	Adults	Home	Backyard	Neighbor-hood	Home Activities Teacher
1.										
2.										
3.										

Key Action Words	Name of Game

Comments: Recommendations for changes, indications of what worked.

FORM 8.12
PARENT SELF-MONITOR FORM

NAME _____ DATE COMPLETED _____

SCHOOL _____ TEACHER _____

Please use this monitor form as a self-check of the activities you implemented. It will help us when we meet and review the implementation of the plan and evaluate the child's progress. If you need more space, use the back of the form. (NA = Not Applicable)

1. Did you implement the plan as intended?	Yes	No	NA
Did you			
. . . review the skill components to be taught?	Yes	No	NA
. . . review the games used in the session?	Yes	No	NA
. . . organize the activities for a short session (3–5 minutes)?	Yes	No	NA
. . . set up the equipment and arrange space before the session?	Yes	No	NA
. . . use the verbal cues (action words) and physical assistance as needed?	Yes	No	NA
. . . provide immediate feedback and encouragement—no failure, only success no matter how small?	Yes	No	NA
. . . eliminate distractions?	Yes	No	NA
. . . record child's progress weekly, or other time as set?	Yes	No	NA
2. Did you call or meet with the teacher if you had concerns?	Yes	No	NA
3. If needed, did you modify the plan for the child?	Yes	No	NA
4. Did you change the objective?	Yes	No	NA
5. Other changes (list below)			

_____

_____

_____

6. Did you meet with the teacher to review and evaluate the plan?	Yes	No	NA
Did you			
. . . examine the child's progress?	Yes	No	NA
. . . determine the child's meaningful gain?	Yes	No	NA
. . . take action based on the child's progress?	Yes	No	NA
If yes, what actions?			

_____

_____

. . . set up a home activities plan for implementation?	Yes	No	NA
. . . set time for next review and implementation?	Yes	No	NA
. . . decide to participate in a parent training program with the teacher?	Yes	No	NA
7. Comments and recommendations (forms, procedures, training, other):			

_____

_____

_____

_____   _____

Signature of Parent   Date Reviewed by Teacher

                                                _____

                                                Signature of Teacher

Social Skills Planning Guide

GETTING STARTED

Social skills are basic for all curricula. Your first planning step is to decide which social skills to teach. You'll then incorporate these skills into the unit plan and adapt the instruction to respond to each child's needs.

Teaching plans often lack a definite statement of a few major social skill objectives and a breakdown of the specific behaviors they entail. But a teacher needs these social skill objectives in order to plan activities that will help the child develop socially acceptable behaviors. These objectives should be based on a knowledge of where each child is and what each child needs.

Social skill objectives, like motor skill objectives, need to be stated in behavioral terms. This requires the objective to be stated in performance terms, setting standards for the child's behavior that

1. accurately reflect the child's behavior as the child progresses toward achieving desired behaviors;
2. accurately reflect what is taught and tested in teaching;
3. provide the teacher with information to plan lessons; and
4. provide the teacher with the effects of instruction—what worked and did not work.

There are three key aspects to consider in planning lessons that involve social skill objectives. First is *the type of game and play involvement.* Planning the lesson to incorporate social skill objectives requires knowledge of learning and playing sequences for the young child. Therefore, you must know the child's level of functioning in play activities and know where the child fits into those sequences.

Initially, the child engages in *solitary play* and learning activities, making no effort to get close to or speak to other children. The child's interest is centered upon a single activity, or the child is entirely passive. Later the child tolerates *parallel play,* that is, another child plays nearby. Yet there is little or no interchange, talking, watching, or lending play materials. As the child develops, interest in the *play of others* (associate play) begins. The child watches the other children and gradually makes advances to enter in their play. The child may borrow or offer to lend play materials or follow another child in a play activity. In this type of play activity, there is no common play or game goal. When the child begins to play in a group that is organized for the purpose of a formal game situation, the child is developing *cooperative play* behaviors.

The second consideration when planning lessons to include social skill objectives is *clear, simple rules and consistent reinforcement.* Some special children have difficulty understanding and following behavioral guidelines in the teaching-learning situation. They may need additional help and guidance. What is important is to expect behavior from these children that is similar to that of children without special needs. The following guidelines have been successful for helping children with special needs:

1. Make rules for behavior simple and easy to understand. Demonstrate and use verbal and nonverbal cues. Be sure the child understands. Have the child demonstrate or verbally show that the rule is understood.
2. Set reasonable limits. You may need to be close to the child in the beginning. Gradually move away, but be sure an adult is in the area.
3. Allow for nondestructive ways of expressing feelings.
4. Have the child understand that angry feelings do

not lead to actions that hurt other people or property. Do not label child "bad" or "naughty" because of the behavior; communicate that it is the behavior, not the child, that is undesirable.

5. Reinforce good behavior. Think positively; praise the child when he or she shows the desired behavior, and help the child correct unacceptable behaviors.

The third consideration is that *social skills are developed naturally* with the right kind of nurturing by the teacher. They are planned and developed primarily through two types of teaching-learning activities:

1. Teacher and learning climate: teacher expectations; positive reinforcement and feedback; motivating activities of high interest to the child; praising child when praise is deserved; taking responsibility for child's learning.

2. Management: simple, clear rules known to the child and consistent reinforcement of rules and consequences; teaching and reviewing rules with children from the beginning of the year; providing active instruction; responding immediately when a problem begins to develop; establishing eye contact with a potentially disruptive child; monitoring for appropriate behavior; signaling inappropriate behavior by using a taught signal or sign to warn child; and active involvement with children for most of class time.

SOCIAL SKILLS

Five social skills are presented in this planning guide:

Following directions

Participating with others

Respecting the rights of others

Task persistence

Independent problem solving

Each social skill is described in behavioral or performance terms, including the goal, the performance objective, the skill components, and related learning skills along with recommended testing procedures and related instructional activities. Individual and Class Records of Progress are provided.

SKILL: FOLLOW DIRECTIONS

Goal

The child will demonstrate understanding and personal social behaviors necessary to learn and play with others.

Performance Objective

The child who is capable of understanding can follow directions in three consecutive class periods, demonstrating the following skill components:

Given the appropriate time, place, situation, or event, the child will follow directions:
1. a nonverbal direction of pointing, motioning to come, or demonstrating the directions;
2. a verbal direction with no more than three repetitions;
3. a verbal direction with no repetition;
4. a two-part direction with no more than three repetitions;
5. a two-part direction with no repetitions; and
6. a set of directions.

Related Learning Skills

The child demonstrates a positive approach to the directions, evidenced by

attempting to follow directions,

asking for help when directions are too difficult,

listening and attending to directions, and

exhibiting one or more of the following behaviors:

eye contact	verbal participation (questions, answers)
head nodding	
hand raising	demonstration—modeling, role playing, pointing, gestures

Recommended Testing Procedures

The skill can be assessed during any of the following teaching and learning situations:

rules and class routines

presentation of the skill

game and play activity—free play or structured play time

During performance, or diagnostic, testing of the child, teaching should not occur.

Related Instructional Activities

Action Words	Games and Play Activities
Follow, look, listen, model, watch, (others added by teacher according to situation selected)	Selected according to direction for child to learn and practice

SKILL: PARTICIPATE WITH OTHERS

Goal

The child will demonstrate personal social behaviors necessary to learn and play with others.

Performance Objective

The child who is capable of understanding can participate with others in three consecutive class periods, demonstrating the following skill components:

Given the appropriate time, place, situation, or event, the child will participate cooperatively with others by
1. choosing to be near other(s),
2. watching and listening to other(s) playing nearby,
3. making a gesture to play with other(s),
4. inviting other(s) to play,
5. responding to positive and negative cues of other(s) by talking, smiling, frowning,
6. choosing to join with other(s) in play,
7. assuming a role in playing with other(s): leader, follower, listener, speaker, helper, and
8. working with other(s) to complete a task to achieve a common goal.

Related Learning Skills

The child demonstrates a positive approach to participating and cooperating with others to achieve a common goal as evidenced by

   listening to others without disruptions or interruptions,

   not complaining or throwing a tantrum when denied role or use of piece of equipment or selection of a specific activity,

   playing in parallel activity with one other child and gradually working with group in associative cooperative play activities,

   volunteering to play with group in associative cooperative activity, and

   volunteering to help other(s) work or play together.

Recommended Testing Procedures

The skill can be assessed during a teaching and learning situation where the child is given the opportunity to play with other(s), such as

   working on the same skill component with other(s) playing games that involve partners or a small group.

During performance, or diagnostic, testing of the child, teaching should not occur.

Related Instructional Activities

Action Words

Identified by teacher according to situation selected

Games and Play Activities

Selected according to type of play: self, partner, group, roles, and positions to play

SKILL: RESPECT THE RIGHTS OF OTHERS

Goal:

The child will demonstrate understanding and personal social behaviors necessary to learn and play with others.

Performance Objective	The child who is capable of understanding can respect the rights of others in three consecutive class periods, demonstrating the following skill components: *Given the appropriate time, place, situation, or event, the child will respect the rights of others by* 1. being willing to take turns using the equipment, 2. being willing to share the equipment, 3. being willing to share the play and work space, 4. asking permission from other(s) to use equipment, 5. receiving approval to use equipment before using it, 6. caring for and using the equipment appropriately, 7. returning equipment within designated time period, 8. returning equipment to designated area or person(s), and 9. helping other(s) to demonstrate acceptable behaviors.

Related Learning Skills

The child demonstrates a positive approach to respecting the rights of others as evidenced by

  volunteering to help keep work area and equipment clean,

  relating appropriate behavior to other(s) through role playing, modeling, and verbalizing,

  demonstrating acceptable behavior, and

  demonstrating acceptable behavior with one another and moving toward doing the same with others in small group activities.

Recommended Testing Procedures

The skill can be assessed during a teaching and learning situation where the child is given the opportunity to play with other(s), such as

  taking turns and sharing space and equipment,

  receiving approval to ask other(s) for equipment and asking permission, and

  caring for and using the equipment, keeping work area clean, and returning equipment.

During performance, or diagnostic, testing of the child, teaching should not occur.

Related Instructional Activities

Action Words	**Games and Play Activities**
Identified by teacher according to situation selected	Selected according to child's responsibilities and type of play: partner, group

SKILL: TASK PERSISTENCE

Goal:

The child will demonstrate understanding and personal social behaviors necessary to learn and play with others.

Performance Objective

The child who is capable of understanding can persevere in three consecutive class periods, demonstrating the following skill components:

Given the appropriate time, place, situation, or event, the child will demonstrate task persistence by
A. attempting task with assistance:
   1. beginning task on time,
   2. working in designated area, and
   3. not interrupting or disrupting other(s);
B. attempting task without assistance:
   4. beginning task on time,
   5. working in designated area, and
   6. not interrupting or disrupting other(s); and
C. completing the task:
   7. asking for help, trying again to complete the task,
   8. completing the task without disrupting other(s), and
   9. completing the task within designated time and space.

Related Learning Skills

The child demonstrates a positive approach to task persistence as evidenced by

   locating and using the necessary equipment for the task,

   returning the equipment to proper location at end of time,

   listening and attending during instructions, and

   not throwing a tantrum when frustrated.

Recommended Testing Procedures

The skill can be assessed during a teaching and learning situation where the child is given a specific task to complete, such as

   skill component to be achieved,

   rules and class routines, or

   game or play activity—free play or structured play time.

During performance, or diagnostic, testing of the child, teaching should not occur.

Related Instructional Activities

Action Words

Work, task, temper, time, help, space (others added by teacher according to situation)

Games and Play Activities

Selected for the child to practice and achieve the motor skill and type of play activity: individual, partner, group

SKILL: INDEPENDENT PROBLEM SOLVING

Goal:

The child will demonstrate understanding and personal social behaviors necessary to learn and play with others.

Performance Objective	The child who is capable of understanding can independently solve problems in three consecutive class periods, demonstrating the following skill components:

Given the appropriate time, place, situation, or event, the child will demonstrate independence in problem solving by
1. identifying skill components or behaviors needed to work on task,
2. making a choice to begin work on the task independently,
3. beginning to work on the task independently by locating and using the appropriate equipment for the task, and then returning it,
4. trying two or more ways (options) to work on the task independently,
5. seeking assistance and knowing when to get help without disrupting others,
6. evaluating successful achievement of the task or the need for further work,
7. using skill or behavior mastered in similar activities, and
8. seeking to help other(s) master the skill or behavior.

Related Learning Skills

The child demonstrates a positive approach to solving problems independently as evidenced by

completing work on a task without regard for feedback for longer periods of time,

demonstrating longer periods of delayed gratification of success while working on task, and

demonstrating longer periods of attention to task.

Recommended Testing Procedures

The skill can be assessed during a teaching and learning situation where the child is given an opportunity to choose a task, such as

skill component to be achieved,

rules and class routines, or

game or play activity—free play or structured play time.

During performance, or diagnostic, testing of the child, teaching should not occur.

Related Instructional Activities

Action Words

Identified by teacher according to situation

Games and Play Activities

Selected by the child

Social Skills Checklists:
Individual and Class Records of Progress

A checklist is an objective score sheet for each social skill taught in the program. By observing and assessing each child's level of performance, you can identify the activities that will assist the child in reaching the performance objective. Use the same checklist to monitor the child's progress during instruction. When the child's performance level changes, you can upgrade the learning tasks (skill components) to the child's new skill level.

To Begin

Decide on one or more activities to be taught in the program. Become familiar with the description of the performance objective for each activity selected. Review the scoring key on the checklist. Plan assessing activities for the selected skills. The number will depend on the class size, the needs of the children, and the help available to you. Set up testing stations similar to the learning stations. Some teachers use free-play time (after setting up equipment for the objective to be tested) to observe the children.

1. Begin assessing at Skill Level 2 for the particular objective. If the child cannot perform at Skill Level 2, assess for Skill Level 1. If the child demonstrates the skill components for Skill Level 2, (i.e., with modeling, verbal cues, or no cues), the child has achieved functional competence. At the next skill level, Skill Level 3, the child demonstrates maintenance retention of the skill over time.

2. For some children with special needs, you may need to assess their levels of functioning before planning teaching activities. As in step 1, observe and assess the amount and type of assistance (cues) the child needs in descending order (i.e., from verbal cues to total manipulation).

Code	Amount and Type of Assistance
SI	Child initiates demonstrating the skill in the teaching and playing of activities
C	Child demonstrates the skill when given verbal cues with or without demonstration
A	Child demonstrates the skill when given partial assistance or total manipulation throughout the execution of the skill

Record, using the code above, the child's initial assistance level and progress in the the comments column of the Class Record of Progress. For some children, this may be the most significant initial progress noted (i.e., from assistance to verbal cues and demonstration).

To Assess

1. Be sure all children are working on objectives at other stations while you are assessing at one station.

2. Set up the testing station beforehand. Make sure that the situation or event planned includes the social skill(s) known to the child or children.

3. Some teachers prefer to observe the child periodically during the regular teaching-learning activities. Note the child's acquisition of the skill components. Then plan activities for the child and evaluate the child's progress.

4. Whatever procedures are selected, be sure the child knows the desired behaviors (i.e., getting and putting equipment away, taking one's place to begin class,

moving from one activity to another, responding to a signal for appropriate behavior, participating with peers, and so forth).

5. You may need to modify the assessing activity for children's special needs by modeling the activity and using sign language or an interpreter. Another modification is an individual assessment with no distractions from other children who are involved in other activities.

To Adapt the Checklists

You can note children's skill components adaptations (i.e., physical devices or other changes) in the comments column on the Class Record of Progress. Other changes can be written under recommendations for individual children or the class. Modifications made for a child can be noted on the Individual Record of Progress. The Class Record of Progress can be adapted for an individual child. Record the name of the child rather than the class, and in the name column, record assessment dates. This adaptation may be needed for children whose progress is erratic, because it provides a base line assessment to find out where to begin teaching and evaluating the child's progress.

The Individual Record of Progress for the end-of-the-year report can be attached to the child's IEP (Individual Education Program) report. The record can also serve as a cumulative record for each child. Such records are very useful for new teachers, substitute teachers, aides, and volunteers, as well as parents. The format of the Individual Record of Progress can also be adapted for a Unit Report. The names of all the objectives for a unit—for example, walk-run endurance, running, catching a ball, and rolling a ball—are written rather than the names of the children. A sample adaptation of the Individual Record of Progress for a child's Unit and Yearly Report is shown in Form 8.7 (pp. 22–25). A sample

adaptation of the Home Activities Report is shown in Form 8.10 (p. 33).

The checklists may be reproduced as needed to implement the play and motor skills program.

CLASS RECORD OF PROGRESS REPORT

CLASS _____ DATE _____

AGE/GRADE _____ TEACHER _____

SCHOOL _____

OBJECTIVE: FOLLOW DIRECTIONS

SCORING:

ASSESSMENT:

_____ Date

X = Achieved

O = Not Achieved

/ = Partially Achieved

REASSESSMENT:

_____ Date

⊗ = Achieved

Ø = Not Achieved

PRIMARY RESPONSES:

N = Not Attending

NR = No Response

UR = Unrelated Response

O = Other (Specify in comments)

NAME	Follows a nonverbal direction.	Follows a verbal direction with no more than three repetitions.	Follows a verbal direction with no repetitions.	Follows a two-part direction with no more than three repetitions.	Follows a two-part direction with no repetitions.	Follows a set of directions.	COMMENTS
	1	2	3	4	5	6	
1.							
2.							
3.							
4.							
5.							
6.							
7.							
8.							
9.							
10.							

Three Consecutive Times

Recommendations: Specific changes or conditions in planning for instructions, performance, or diagnostic testing procedures or standards. Please describe what worked best.

_____

_____

_____

_____

_____

CLASS RECORD OF PROGRESS REPORT

CLASS _____   DATE _____

AGE/GRADE _____   TEACHER _____

SCHOOL _____

OBJECTIVE: PARTICIPATE WITH OTHERS

SCORING:	Three Consecutive Times								PRIMARY RESPONSES:
ASSESSMENT: _____Date **X** = Achieved **O** = Not Achieved **/** = Partially Achieved REASSESSMENT: _____Date **Ø** = Achieved **Ø** = Not Achieved	Chooses to be near other(s).	Watches and listens to other(s) playing nearby.	Makes a gesture to play with others.	Invites other(s) to play.	Responds to positive and negative cues of other(s) by talking, smiling, frowning.	Chooses to join with other(s) in play.	Assumes a role in playing with other(s): leader, follower, listener, speaker, helper.	Works with other(s) to complete a task to achieve common goal.	N = Not Attending NR = No Response UR = Unrelated Response O = Other (Specify in comments)
NAME	1	2	3	4	5	6	7	8	COMMENTS
1.									
2.									
3.									
4.									
5.									
6.									
7.									
8.									
9.									
10.									

Recommendations: Specific changes or conditions in planning for instructions, performance, or diagnostic testing procedures or standards. Please describe what worked best.

_____

_____

_____

_____

_____

Class Record of Progress Report

CLASS _____   DATE _____

AGE/GRADE _____   TEACHER _____

SCHOOL _____

OBJECTIVE: RESPECT THE RIGHTS OF OTHERS

SCORING:

ASSESSMENT:

_____Date

X = Achieved

O = Not Achieved

/ = Partially Achieved

REASSESSMENT:

_____Date

⊗ = Achieved

Ø = Not Achieved

PRIMARY RESPONSES:

N = Not Attending

NR = No Response

UR = Unrelated Response

O = Other (Specify in comments)

NAME	Takes turns using the equipment.	Shares the equipment.	Shares the play and work space.	Asks permission from other(s) to use equipment.	Receives approval to use equipment before using it.	Cares for and uses the equipment appropriately.	Returns equipment within designated time period.	Returns equipment to designated area or person(s).	Helps other(s) to demonstrate acceptable behaviors.	COMMENTS
	1	2	3	4	5	6	7	8	9	
1.										
2.										
3.										
4.										
5.										
6.										
7.										
8.										
9.										
10.										

Recommendations: Specific changes or conditions in planning for instructions, performance, or diagnostic testing procedures or standards. Please describe what worked best.

_____

_____

_____

_____

_____

CLASS RECORD OF PROGRESS REPORT

CLASS _____   DATE _____

AGE/GRADE _____   TEACHER _____

SCHOOL _____

OBJECTIVE: TASK PERSISTENCE

SCORING: ASSESSMENT: _____Date X = Achieved O = Not Achieved / = Partially Achieved REASSESSMENT: _____Date ⊗ = Achieved ∅ = Not Achieved	Three Consecutive Times									PRIMARY RESPONSES: N = Not Attending NR = No Response UR = Unrelated Response O = Other (Specify in comments)
NAME	Attempts task with assistance and begins task on time.	Attempts task with assistance and works in designated area.	Attempts task with assistance and does not disrupt other(s).	Attempts task without assistance and begins task on time.	Attempts task without assistance and works in designated area.	Attempts task without assistance and does not disrupt other(s).	Asks for help, tries again to complete task.	Completes task without disrupting other(s).	Completes task within designated time and space.	COMMENTS
	1	2	3	4	5	6	7	8	9	
1.										
2.										
3.										
4.										
5.										
6.										
7.										
8.										
9.										
10.										

Recommendations: Specific changes or conditions in planning for instructions, performance, or diagnostic testing procedures or standards. Please describe what worked best.

_____

_____

_____

_____

_____

CLASS RECORD OF PROGRESS REPORT

CLASS _____   DATE _____

AGE/GRADE _____   TEACHER _____

SCHOOL _____

OBJECTIVE: INDEPENDENT PROBLEM SOLVING

SCORING: ASSESSMENT: _____Date **X** = Achieved **O** = Not Achieved / = Partially Achieved REASSESSMENT: _____Date **⊗** = Achieved **Ø** = Not Achieved					Three Consecutive Times					PRIMARY RESPONSES: N = Not Attending NR = No Response UR = Unrelated Response O = Other (Specify in comments)
NAME	Identifies skill components or behaviors needed to work on task.	Makes a choice to begin work on task independently.	Begins to work on task independently by locating and using appropriate equipment, and then returning it.	Tries two or more ways (options) to work on task independently.	Seeks assistance and knows when to get help without disrupting other(s).	Evaluates successful achievement of the task or the need for further work.	Uses skill or behavior mastered in similar activities.	Seeks to help other(s) master the skill or behavior.	COMMENTS
	1	2	3	4	5	6	7	8	
1.									
2.									
3.									
4.									
5.									
6.									
7.									
8.									
9.									
10.									

Recommendations: Specific changes or conditions in planning for instructions, performance, or diagnostic testing procedures or standards. Please describe what worked best.

_____

_____

_____

_____

_____

INDIVIDUAL RECORD OF PROGRESS

Area: Social Skills

CHILD: _____

LEVEL: _____

YEAR: _____

TEACHER: _____

SCHOOL: _____

Marking Period	*Date*
Fall Conference (white)	from____to____
Winter Conference (yellow)	from____to____
Spring Conference (pink)	from____to____
End-of-Year (cumulative) Report (blue)	from____to____

Preprimary Play and Motor Skills Activity Program

The Individual Record of Progress lists all of the objectives in which your child receives instruction during the play and motor skills program. The information reported on your child's Individual Record of Progress shows your child's entry performance and progress for a marking period. The end-of-the-year report represents your child's Individual Education Program (IEP) for the objectives selected and taught during the year.

Each objective is broken into small, measurable steps or skill components. This assists the teacher to assess what your child already knew before teaching began and to determine which step to start teaching first. One of the following symbols is marked by each step or skill component of the objective:

X = The child already knew how to perform this step before teaching it began.

O = The child did not know how to perform this step before teaching it began or after instruction of it ended.

Ø = The child did not know how to perform this step before teaching it began, but did learn how to do it during the instruction period.

This information should be helpful to you in planning home activities to strengthen your child's play and motor skills.

Comments

_____

_____

_____

_____

_____

_____

_____

_____

FOLLOW DIRECTIONS

Date: _____

Three consecutive class periods

—— Follows a nonverbal direction.

—— Follows a verbal direction with no more than three repetitions.

—— Follows a verbal direction with no repetitions.

—— Follows a two-part direction with no more than three repetitions.

—— Follows a two-part direction with no repetitions.

—— Follows a set of directions.

PARTICIPATE WITH OTHERS

Date: _____

Three consecutive class periods

—— Chooses to be near other(s).

—— Watches and listens to other(s) playing nearby.

—— Makes a gesture to play with other(s).

—— Invites other(s) to play.

—— Responds to positive and negative cues of other(s) by talking, smiling, frowning.

—— Chooses to join with other(s) in play.

—— Assumes a role in playing with other(s).

—— Works with other(s) to achieve a common goal.

RESPECT THE RIGHTS OF OTHERS

Date: _____

Three consecutive class periods

—— Takes turns using the equipment.

—— Shares the equipment.

—— Shares the play and work space.

—— Asks permission from other(s) to use equipment.

—— Receives approval to use equipment before using it.

—— Cares for and uses the equipment appropriately.

—— Returns equipment within designated time period.

—— Returns equipment to designed area or person(s).

—— Helps other(s) to demonstrate acceptable behaviors.

TASK PERSISTENCE

Date: _____

Three consecutive class periods
Attempts task with assistance

____ Begins task on time.

____ Works in designated area.

____ Does not interrupt or disrupt others.

Attempts task without assistance

____ Begins task on time.

____ Works in designated area.

____ Does not interrupt or disrupt others.

Completes the task

____ Asks for help, tries again to complete task.

____ Completes task without disrupting other(s).

____ Completes task within designated time and space.

INDEPENDENT PROBLEM SOLVING

Date: _____

Three consecutive class periods

____ Identifies skill components or behaviors needed to work on task.

____ Makes a choice to begin work on task independently.

____ Begins to work on task independently by locating and using the appropriate equipment for the task, and then returning it.

____ Tries two or more ways (options) to work on task independently.

____ Seeks assistance and knows when to get help without disrupting other(s).

____ Evaluates successful achievement of the task or the need for further work.

____ Uses skill or behavior mastered in similar activities.

____ Seeks to help other(s) master the skill or behavior.

APPENDIX A:
PLANNING WORKSHEETS FOR TEACHING

Worksheet 1:   Selecting Instructional Objectives by Goal Area

Worksheet 2:   Instructional Time and Total Number of Objectives to Be Included in the Program

Worksheet 3:   Essential Objectives by Goal Area for the School Year

Worksheet 4:   The Teaching Unit Plan: Yearly Program

Sample   The Teaching Unit Plan: Yearly Program

Worksheet 5:   Teaching Unit Lesson Plan

Worksheet 6:   Unit Games and Play Activity Plan

Worksheet 7:   Lesson Plan

Worksheet 8:   Action Words

WORKSHEET 1:
SELECTING INSTRUCTIONAL OBJECTIVES BY GOAL AREA

Directions: Check (√) all objectives you would like to include in the program for this year. Then write in a priority rating of 1, 2, or 3 beside each objective selected. Write in additional objectives by the appropriate goal area. If there is more than one teacher, reproduce this sheet and use as a summary worksheet.

TEACHER _____

CLASS/AGE LEVEL _____

SCHOOL _____

YEAR _____

1. LOCOMOTOR AND RHYTHMIC SKILLS	2. BALL-HANDLING SKILLS	3. HEALTH AND FITNESS SKILLS	4. PLAY SKILLS	5. BODY MANAGEMENT AND STUNTS AND TUMBLING SKILLS	6. SOCIAL SKILLS
____ Slide	____ Roll a ball	____ Situps (abdominal strength)	____ Hang from a bar	____ Body parts	____ Follow directions
____ Run	____ Throw a ball	____ Walk-run for endurance	____ Push and pull object	____ Body actions	____ Participate with others
____ Jump	____ Bounce a ball	____ Trunk and leg flexibility	____ Ride a tricycle or bicycle	____ Shapes and sizes	____ Respect rights of others
____ Hop	____ Catch a ball	____ Lift and carry objects	____ Swing on a swing	____ Use of space	____ Task persistence
____ Climb	____ Kick a ball	____ Rest and relaxation	____ Slide down a slide	____ Directions in space	____ Independent problem solving
____ Skip	____ Hit a ball	____ Other (list)	____ Travel on a scooterboard	____ Log roll	____ Other (list)
____ Gallop	____ Other (list)		____ Other (list)	____ Forward roll	
____ Even beat				____ Backward roll	
____ Uneven beat				____ Static balance	
____ Accent				____ Dynamic balance	
____ Expressive movement				____ Parachute	
____ Singing games				____ Other (list)	
____ Other (list)					

When objectives have been selected, go to Worksheet 2.

WORKSHEET 2:
INSTRUCTIONAL TIME AND TOTAL NUMBER OF OBJECTIVES TO BE INCLUDED IN THE PROGRAM

Directions: Use your school calendar to complete the following calculations for determining the amount of time that is available for instruction during the school year.

TEACHER _____

CLASS/AGE LEVEL _____

SCHOOL _____

YEAR _____

1. Determine the total number of minutes available per year for instruction.

A. Total number of instructional weeks in year's program = _____ weeks
   (Excluding Christmas, spring, and summer vacations, a 180-day school year has 36 instructional weeks, and a 230-day school year has 47 instructional weeks.)

B. Number of weeks of canceled classes (due to conferences, psychological testing, swimming schedule, snow days, field trips, election days when gym is in use, holiday assemblies, beginning and ending of school, and so on) = _____ weeks

C. Number of weeks of "flex time" (adjustments to allow for additional unplanned instructional needs) = _____ weeks

D. Number of weeks per year actually available for instruction (A minus B and C) = _____ weeks

$$
\begin{array}{rl}
 & \underline{\hspace{3cm}} \ \text{(A)} \\
- & \underline{\hspace{3cm}} \ \text{(B)} \\
 & \underline{\hspace{3cm}} \\
- & \underline{\hspace{3cm}} \ \text{(C)} \\
 & \underline{\hspace{3cm}} \ \text{(D)}
\end{array}
$$

E. Number of gym classes per week = _____ gym classes

F. Number of minutes per gym class available for instruction (excluding dressing and set-up time) = _____ minutes

G. Number of gym minutes actually available for instruction per year (D x E x F) = _____ minutes

$$
\begin{array}{rl}
 & \underline{\hspace{3cm}} \ \text{(D)} \\
\times & \underline{\hspace{3cm}} \ \text{(E)} \\
 & \underline{\hspace{3cm}} \\
\times & \underline{\hspace{3cm}} \ \text{(F)} \\
 & \underline{\hspace{3cm}} \ \text{(G)}
\end{array}
$$

2. Determine total number of minutes needed for children to achieve meaningful gain on one objective (two or more skill components).

H. Estimate average number of minutes needed to achieve one objective (based on time line below; see also p. 6) = _____ minutes

120 minutes	180 minutes	240 minutes	360 minutes
Δ	Δ	Δ	Δ
Higher Functioning			Slower Functioning
Faster Learner			Slower Learner

3. Determine total number of objectives that can be included in one year.

I. Divide number of instructional minutes available by number of minutes needed to achieve one objective (G ÷ H) = _____ objectives per year

(G) _____ / _____ (H) = _____ (I)

4. Determine total number of objectives for multiyear program.

J. Multiply I by number of years of program = _____ objectives

WORKSHEET 3:
ESSENTIAL OBJECTIVES BY GOAL AREA FOR THE SCHOOL YEAR

Directions: Determine the percentage of emphasis for each goal area and record. Calculate the number of objectives per goal area (% of emphasis x total number of objectives for year) and record. Review Worksheet 1, and select priority objectives for each goal area according to the number of objectives calculated for it.

TEACHER _____

CLASS/AGE LEVEL _____

SCHOOL _____

YEAR _____

GOAL AREA	% OF EMPHASIS	# OF OBJECTIVES	PRIORITY OBJECTIVES
1. Locomotor and Rhythmic Skills			
2. Ball-Handling Skills			
3. Health and Fitness Skills			
4. Play Skills (equipment)			
5. Body Management and Stunts and Tumbling Skills			
6. Social Skills			

Remember: Games are used to teach the specific instructional objective or skill.

WORKSHEET 4:
THE TEACHING UNIT PLAN: YEARLY PROGRAM

Directions: Complete the information below. On the basis of Worksheet 3, group the objectives into teaching unit plans. Sequence the units for the year. Assign time (minutes) for each unit and objective. The time assignments should add up to the total minutes needed for meaningful gain and the number of weeks recorded on Worksheet 2.

UNIT PLAN (#):	INSTRUCTIONAL OBJECTIVES	MINUTES	WEEKS

SAMPLE:
THE TEACHING UNIT PLAN: YEARLY PROGRAM

In developing a yearly program plan of units of instruction, eight objectives were selected from the long-term scope and sequence chart for emphasis during the year. Actual instruction time: 200 minutes for meaningful gain per objective = 3,200 minutes.

> 5 days/week x 20 minutes/day = 100 minutes/week
>
> 100 minutes/week x 4 weeks/unit = 400 minutes/unit
>
> 3,200 minutes/year ÷ 400 minutes/unit = 8 units/year

Unit Plan (#)	Instructional Objectives	Minutes	Weeks
1.	Follow Directions	80	
	Situps (abdominal strength)	60	
	Walk-Run Endurance	60	
	Roll a Ball	100	
	Catch a Ball	100 (400)	4
2.	Follow Directions	40	
	Playground Skills	240	
	Slide and Swing		
	Travel on a Scooterboard		
	Walk on a Balance Beam (dynamic balance)	120 (400)	4
3.	Follow Directions	40	
	Personal Space	120	
	Walk on a Balance Beam	120	
	Roll a Ball	60	
	Catch a Ball	60 (400)	4
4.	Follow Directions	40	
	Personal Space	120	
	Roll a Ball	40	
	Catch a Ball	40	
	Walk on a Balance Beam	60	
	Fitness (see 2 POs above)	120 (400)	4
5.	Personal Space	80	
	Fitness (see above 2 POs)	80	
	Body Parts	100	
	Climbing	100	
	General Space	40 (400)	4
6.	General Space	100	
	Body Parts	50	
	Climbing	50	
	Even Beat	100	
	Running	100 (400)	4
7.	General Space	100	
	Directions in Space	80	
	Body Parts	50	
	Climbing	50	
	Even Beat	60	
	Running	60 (400)	4
8.	Directions in Space	120	
	Playground Skills (see 2 POs above)	80	
	Even Beat	40	
	Running	40	
	Respect Rights of Others	120 (400)	4
		3,200 minutes	32 weeks

WORKSHEET 5:
TEACHING UNIT LESSON PLAN

Directions: Complete the information below. Develop the Unit Lesson Plan for Unit 1 developed in Worksheet 4.

Projected Timeline: _____ to _____

Objectives: _____

Teacher: _____   School: _____

Gym Days/Times: _____   Level: _____

WORKSHEET 6:
UNIT GAMES AND PLAY ACTIVITY PLAN

Directions: Review the games for the instructional objectives that make up Unit 1. Select the games that you decide to use in teaching the activities/skills.

Unit No.: _____   Level: _____   Objective: _____

ACTIVITY	ORGANIZATION	DESCRIPTION/INSTRUCTIONS	EQUIPMENT

WORKSHEET 7:
LESSON PLAN

Unit Plan _____ Date _____ Class _____ Time _____

Equipment _____

PHASE	ACTIVITY	TIME
Introductory Activity		
Lesson Body		
Summary		

WORKSHEET 8:
ACTION WORDS

Directions: Select key Action Words to use in teaching the performance objectives.

ACTION WORDS
Actions:
Objects:
Concepts:

ACTION WORDS
Actions:
Objects:
Concepts:

ACTION WORDS
Actions:
Objects:
Concepts:

ACTION WORDS
Actions:
Objects:
Concepts:

ACTION WORDS
Actions:
Objects:
Concepts:

APPENDIX B:
PLANNING WORKSHEETS FOR HOME ACTIVITIES PROGRAM

Worksheet 1:   Parent Questionnaire: The Instructional Plan

Worksheet 2:   Interview Form: Home Information Sheet

Worksheet 3:   Weekly Home Activities Log Plan

Worksheet 4:   Action Words

Worksheet 5:   Games Selected

Worksheet 1:
Parent Questionnaire: The Instructional Plan

Please check (√) for your child in the appropriate column opposite each performance objective selected for the yearly program plan.

Year _____

Date _____

Essential Performance Objectives (Skills) Planned	Can Do	Needs More Help to Do Well	Needs to Learn to Do
1.			
2.			
3.			
4.			
5.			
6.			
7.			
8.			
9.			
10.			

Comments: Please list other play and motor skills you wish your child to learn. _____

_____

_____

_____

WORKSHEET 2:
INTERVIEW FORM: HOME INFORMATION SHEET

CHILD'S NAME _____   AGE _____

RELATIONSHIP TO CHILD _____   INTERVIEW DATE _____

Interviewer: Complete the parent questionnaire (sent with letter). Then begin with these questions:

---

1. WHO IS THE PRIMARY CARE-GIVER FOR YOUR CHILD?
   a. Mother   d. Brother
   b. Father   e. Sister
   c. Babysitter   f. Other _____

2. HOW MUCH TIME DOES PRIMARY CARE-GIVER HAVE TO PLAY WITH YOUR CHILD EACH DAY?
   a. 15 minutes   c. 60 minutes
   b. 30 minutes   d. Other _____

3. WOULD YOU BE WILLING TO PARTICIPATE IN A HOME MOTOR SKILLS AND PLAY ACTIVITY PROGRAM FOR YOU AND YOUR CHILD?
   Yes _____   No _____

4. IF NO, WHY NOT? _____
   _____

5. IF YES, WHEN DO YOU WISH TO BEGIN? DATE: _____

6. HOW MUCH TIME WOULD YOU BE WILLING TO DEVOTE TO IT AS YOU BEGIN?
   Days per week (no.) _____   Minutes per day _____

PLAY AND GAME ACTIVITIES: HOME, NEIGHBORHOOD

What game and play activities does your child now participate in, with whom, and where? What would you like your child to be able to do in the future? (Focus on performance objectives taught in instruction.)

ACTIVITIES NOW	WITH WHOM?	WHERE?	FUTURE ACTIVITIES

WORKSHEET 3:
WEEKLY HOME ACTIVITIES LOG PLAN

NAME _____ TEACHER _____ PHONE _____

PERFORMANCE OBJECTIVE _____ DATE GIVEN _____ DATE RECEIVED _____

WEEKLY PLAN _____

PARENT NAME _____ PARENT PHONE _____

WEEK	DATES	TIMES A DAY	MINUTES	ALONE	OTHER CHILDREN	ADULTS	HOME	BACKYARD	NEIGHBOR-HOOD	HOME ACTIVITIES TEACHER
1.										
2.										
3.										

Key Action Words	Name of Game

Comments: Recommendations for changes, indications of what worked.

WORKSHEET 4:
ACTION WORDS

Directions: Select key Action Words to use in teaching the performance objectives.

ACTION WORDS
Actions:
Objects:
Concepts:

ACTION WORDS
Actions:
Objects:
Concepts:

ACTION WORDS
Actions:
Objects:
Concepts:

ACTION WORDS
Actions:
Objects:
Concepts:

ACTION WORDS
Actions:
Objects:
Concepts:

WORKSHEET 5:
GAMES SELECTED

Directions: Select the games you plan to use for the skills to be taught. Complete this worksheet. It will help you plan daily activities.

SKILLS	GAME	ORGANIZATION	DESCRIPTION/INSTRUCTIONS	EQUIPMENT

APPENDIX C:
MASTER LIST OF ACTION WORDS

Key: The letter A, O, or C after each word indicates whether it is used as an Action, an Object, or a Concept. The number (or numbers) after each word is the number of the book in which it is used.

Abdominal region (O, 6)

Across (C, 2, 3)

Afraid (C, 5)

Angry (C, 5)

Ankle (O, 5)

Arm (O, 1, 2, 3, 4, 6, 7)

Around (C, 1, 6, 7)

Away (C, 5)

Away from (C, 6)

Back (C, 2, 3, 4, 5)

Back (O, 3, 4, 6, 7)

Backward (C, 2, 3, 4, 6, 7)

Bake (A, 5)

Balance (A, 3)

Balance beam (O, 3)

Balance board (O, 3)

Ball (O, 2, 3, 5, 6)

Balloon (O, 2)

Bar (O, 7)

Barrel (O, 1, 3)

Bases (O, 4)

Beam (O, 1)

Beanbag (O, 2, 3, 6)

Beat (C, 5)

Bed (O, 5)

Behind (C, 1, 2, 6, 7)

Bell (O, 1)

Belly (O, 7)

Bench (O, 4)

Bend (A, 1, 2, 3, 4, 6, 7)

Beside (C, 6, 7)

Between (C, 1, 2, 3, 6, 7)

Big (C, 6)

Bike (O, 7)

Blade (O, 2)

Blanket (O, 3)

Blink (A, 5)

Block (O, 4, 7)

Board (O, 1, 3)

Body (O, 6)

Book (O, 7)

Both (C, 1, 2, 4)

Bottom (C, 6, 7)

Bottom (seat) (O, 6)

Bounce (A, 2)

Boundaries (C, 6)

Box (O, 2, 4, 7)

Boxes (O, 2)

Boy (O, 1)

Breathing (A, 4)

Bumped (A, 5, 7)

By (C, 6)

Cake (O, 5)

Carry (A, 4)

Catch (A, 2, 5)

Ceiling (O, 6)

Center (C, 3)

Chair (O, 1, 2, 3)

Chest (O, 6)

Chin (O, 3, 4, 6)

Circle (O, 1)

Clap (A, 5)

Clasp (A, 5)

Climb (A, 1, 7)

Clock (O, 5)

Close (A, 5)

Close (C, 4)

Come back (A, 5)

Cone (O, 1, 2, 5)

Contact (C, 2)

Control (A, 1, 4)

Corners (O, 6)

Crawl (A, 1, 5)

Crawled (A, 5)

Crocodile (O, 5)

Cup (O, 5)

Curl (A, 4)

Curved (C, 6)

Down (C, 1–7)

Do this (C, 1, 5)

Drink (A, 5)

Drum (O, 4, 5)

Edge (O, 2)

Elbow (O, 6)

Erect (C, 1)

Even (C, 5)

Extend (A, 3)

Eyes (O, 2, 4, 6)

Face (O, 4)

Far (C, 6)

Fast (C, 1, 3, 4, 5)

Feel (C, 4)

Feet (foot) (O, 1–7)

Fell (A, 5)

Fingers (O, 2, 4, 5, 6)

Fist (O, 4)

Flat (C, 4)

Fly away (A, 5)

Floor (O, 4, 6, 7)

Follow (A, 7)

Footprints (O, 3, 4)

Forth (C, 5)

Forward (C, 1, 2, 3, 4, 6, 7)

Frog (O, 5)

Front (C, 1, 3, 4, 6)

Gallop (A, 1, 5)

Geometric shapes (O, 3)

Girl (O, 1)

Go (A, 1, 3, 4, 5, 7)

Grasp (A, 2, 3, 4, 7)

Grip (A, 7)

Ground (O, 7)

Hang (A, 7)

Hand (O, 1–7)

Handlebars (O, 7)

Handrail (O, 1)

Happy (C, 5)

Hard (C, 2, 4, 5, 7)

Head (O, 2, 3, 6)

Hear (C, 1)

High (C, 1, 7)

Hill (O, 5)

Hips (O, 6)

Hit (A, 2)

Hockey stick (O, 2)

Hold (A, 1, 2, 3, 4, 7)

Hoops (O, 2)

Hop (A, 1, 5)

House (O, 5)

In (C, 6)

In front of (C, 6)

Inside (C, 6)

Jump (A, 1)

Jumping (A, 5)

Jungle gym (O, 6)

Kick (A, 2)

Knead (A, 5)

Knee (O, 3, 4, 6, 7)

Kneel (A, 1, 3, 7)

Ladder (O, 1)

Land (A, 1, 3)

Large (C, 6)

Lead (C, 1)

Lead foot (O, 1)

Lean (A, 4, 7)

Left (C, 1, 6, 7)

Leg (O, 1, 2, 3, 4, 6, 7)

Lend (A, 3)

Let go (C, 4)

Lie (A, 4, 6, 7)

Lift (A, 1, 2, 3, 4, 7)

Lift up (A, 7)

Line (O, 1, 2, 3, 4, 7)

Long (C, 6)

Look (C, 1–7)

Loud (C, 5)

Low (C, 7)

Lower (C, 2, 4, 6)

Man (O, 5)

March (A, 5)

Mat (O, 1, 3, 4)

Middle (C, 3)

Monkey (O, 5)

More (C, 2)

Move (A, 1–7)

Mushroom (O, 3)

Narrow (C, 6)

Near (C, 1, 6)

No (C, 1, 6)

Nose (O, 6)

Numbers (1–6) (C, 5)

Obstacles (O, 7)

Of (C, 5)

Off (C, 3, 5, 7)

On (C, 1, 2, 3, 7)

One (C, 2)

Open (C, 5)

Other (C, 1)

Out (C, 1, 5, 6)

Outside (C, 6)

Over (C, 1, 3, 6, 7)

Overhead (C, 3)

Pail (O, 2)

Palms (O, 3)

Parachute (O, 3)

Partner (O, 5)

Path (O, 1)

Pedal (O, 7)

Personal (C, 6)

Phone (O, 5)

Phoned (A, 5)

Piano (O, 5)

Pick up (A, 4)

Picture (O, 3)

Picture of daily activities (O, 5)

Picture of feelings (O, 5)

Picture of recreation activity (O, 5)

Pinkie (O, 5)

Pins (O, 7)

Place (A, 7)

Play (A, 5)

Play area (O, 6)

Playground (O, 6)

Playroom (O, 6)

Pocket (O, 5)

Point (A, 6, 7)

Pot (O, 5)

Pour (A, 5)

Pretend (C, 5)

Pull (A, 1, 3, 7)

Pump (A, 7)

Push (A, 2, 3, 7)

Push toy (O, 2)

Put (A, 5)

Put down (A, 4)

Rabbit (O, 5)

Railing (O, 1)

Rails (O, 4)

Raise (A, 3, 4, 6)

Reach (A, 2, 3, 4, 6)

Ready (C, 1–7)

Ready position (C, 3)

Rear (C, 1, 3)

Rear foot (O, 1)

Records (O, 5)

Relax (A, 4)

Release (A, 2, 6)

Return (A, 4)

Ride (A, 7)

Right (C, 1, 6)

Ring (O, 5)

Ring man (O, 5)

Ripple (A, 3)

Roll (A, 2, 3, 5)

Rope (0, 6, 7)

Round (C, 3)

Run (A, 1, 4, 5)

Sad (C, 5)

Saw (A, 5)

Say (A, 6)

Scooterboard (O, 6, 7)

Seat (bottom) (O, 6, 7)

Serve (A, 2)

Short (C, 6)

Shoulder (O, 3, 4)

Shout (A, 5)

Show (A, 6)

Show me (C, 1–7)

Shut (C, 5)

Side (C, 3, 4)

Side (O, 2, 7)

Sideways (C, 1, 2, 6, 7)

Singing (A, 5)

Sit (A, 1, 2, 4, 5, 6, 7)

Skip (A, 1, 5)

Slide (A, 1, 5, 6, 7)

Slow (C, 4, 5)

Slowly (C, 4)

Small (C, 6)

Space (C, 6)

Spider (O, 5)

Spout (O, 5)

Squat (A, 3)

Squeeze tight (A, 4)

Stairs (O, 1)

Stamp (A, 5)

Stand (A, 1, 2, 3, 4, 6, 7)

Start (A, 4)

Step (A, 1, 2, 3, 4, 5, 7)

Step (O, 1)

Step down (A, 1)

Step-hop (A, 1)

Step up (A, 1)

Stick (O, 4, 5, 6)

Stomach (O, 6)

Stones (O, 2)

Stood (A, 5)

Stop (A, 1, 2, 3, 4, 7)

Straddle (A, 3)

Straight (C, 3, 4, 6, 7)

Straighten (A, 6)

Sun (O, 5)

Surface (ground) (O, 6)

Sway (A, 6)

Swing (A, 1, 2, 6, 7)

Swing (O, 6, 7)

Tall (C, 5)

Tall man (O, 5)

Tap (A, 5)

Tape (O, 4)

Tapes (O, 5)

Target (O, 2)

Tense (A, 4)

Thigh (upper leg) (O, 6)

Through (C, 1, 2, 6)

Throw (A, 2, 5)

Thumbkin (O, 4)

Thump (A, 5)

Tight (C, 3, 4)

Time (C, 5)

To (C, 1, 2)

Toes (O, 2, 3, 4, 6)

Together (C, 1, 3, 5)

Top (C, 6, 7)

Touch (A, 6, 7)

Toward (C, 2, 6)

Toy (O, 1, 3, 4, 7)

Tuck (A, 3, 4)

Turn (A, 1, 3, 6, 7)

Trunk (O, 1, 4, 6)

Twist (A, 6)

Umbrella (O, 3)

Uncurl (A, 4)

Under (C, 1, 2, 6, 7)

Uneven (C, 5)

Up (C, 1–7)

Upper (C, 1, 2, 3, 6)

Wagon (O, 7)

Walk (A, 1, 2, 4, 5, 7)

Wall (O, 2, 6)

Wane (A, 5)

Wash (A, 5)

Watch (A, 1, 5)

Water spout (O, 5)

Weight (C, 2)

Whistle (C, 1)

Wide (C, 5, 6)

Width (sides) (C, 6)

Wink (A, 5)

Yardstick (O, 4, 5)

Yes (C, 5)

Appendix D:
Master List of Games Matched to Objective

Games*	Performance Objective	Book
Animal Track (7)	Hopping, Jumping	1
Around the World (9)	Walk-Run for Endurance	4
Around We Go (4)	Move to Even Beat, Accent	5
A Tiny Little Mouse (7)	Expressive Communication	5
A-tisket, A-tasket (7)	Expressive Communication, Singing Games	5
Baa Baa Black Sheep (4)	Move to Even Beat, Expressive Communication, Singing Games	5
Balancing Fun (9)	Static Balancing	3
Ball in Self Space (9)	Personal Space	6
Ball in the Basket (8)	Rolling, Catching, Throwing, and Kicking a Ball	2
Balloon Push (7)	Push and Pull Object	7
Ball Pass Relay (3)	Rolling and Throwing a Ball	2
Base Running (8)	Galloping, Hopping, Jumping, Running, Skipping, Sliding	1
Bat Ball (9)	Hitting a Ball	2
Beanbag Relay (9)	Dynamic Balancing	3
Beat the Stars (9)	Situps	4
Big and Small (9)	Shapes and Sizes	6
Bike Relay (8)	Ride Tricycle or Bicycle	7
Birds, Beasts, and Fish (5)	Body Parts	6
Body Tag (4)	Body Parts	6
Bounce Ball Relay (9)	Bouncing a Ball	2
Boundary Ball (8)	Throwing, Catching, and Bouncing a Ball	2
Bowling Game (9)	Rolling, Throwing, Kicking, and Hitting a Ball	2
Brother John (4)	Move to Even Beat, Expressive Communication, Singing Games	5

* Number in parentheses refers to source of games. The numbered list of game sources is at the end of this appendix. Although only one source is identified for each game, many games are found in a number of the sources.

GAMES	PERFORMANCE OBJECTIVE	BOOK
Bunny Hop (7)	Expressive Communication, Singing Games	5
Busy Bee (10)	Body Actions	6
Cageball Push (7)	Push and Pull Object	7
Cageball Roll and Push (7)	Rolling a Ball	2
Call Ball (1)	Throwing, Catching, and Kicking a Ball	2
Capture the Bacon (6)	Parachute	3
Car Races (9)	Parachute	3
Catch a Falling Star (7)	Expressive Communication, Singing Games	5
Catching Balloons and Soap Bubbles (7)	Catching a Ball	2
Catching Fish (7)	Galloping, Hopping, Jumping, Running, Skipping, Sliding	1
Cat and Rat (4)	Parachute	3
Circle Strike Ball (8)	Travel on Scooterboard	7
Circle Tag (8)	Galloping, Hopping, Jumping, Running, Skipping, Sliding	1
Cleaning Out the Backyard (9)	Throwing a Ball	2
Climbing Hills, Paths (7)	Climbing Stairs	1
Climbing Over Snowbanks (7)	Climbing Stairs	1
Climbing Races (7)	All Locomotor Skills	1
Climbing Ropes, Frames (7)	Climbing Stairs	1
Color Pick-up (5)	Parachute	3
Count to Six Fast (9)	Move to Even Beat	5
Crocodile Song (7)	Expressive Communication, Singing Games	5
Crossing the Lake (3)	Jumping	1
Diamond Relay (9)	Rolling and Kicking a Ball	2
Diddle Diddle Dumpling (4)	Move to Even Beat, Expressive Communication, Singing Games	5

GAMES	PERFORMANCE OBJECTIVE	BOOK
Did You Ever See a Lassie/Laddie? (8)	Hang from Bar, Push and Pull Object, Ride Tricycle or Bicycle, Swing on Swing, Travel on Scooterboard, Slide Down Slide	7
Discovering Directions (9)	Directions in Space	6
Do As I Do (7)	Sliding	1
Do This, Do That (7)	All Body Movement and Play Skills	6, 7
Drop the Flag (9)	Galloping, Hopping, Running, Skipping	1
Duck Duck Goose (1)	Galloping, Running, Skipping	1
Eensy Weensy Spider (7)	Expressive Communication, Singing Games	5
Endurance Course (9)	Walk-Run for Endurance	4
Even-Uneven Tempo Relay (9)	Move to Even and Uneven Beats	5
Fast and Slow (9)	Sliding	1
Figure 8 Run (9)	Walk-Run for Endurance	4
Find the Figure (5)	Parachute	3
Fish Net (7)	Running	1
Five Green Speckled Frogs (7)	Expressive Communication, Singing Games	5
Five Little Chickadees (5)	All Rhythmic Skills	5
Five Little Monkeys (7)	Expressive Communication, Singing Games	5
Flash Cards	Body Parts	6
Floor Hockey (7)	Hitting a Ball	2
Follow the Ball (4)	Sliding	1
Follow the Drum (9)	Move to Even and Uneven Beats, Accent	5
Follow the Drum Beat (9)	Dynamic Balancing	3
Follow the Leader (1)	All Play Skills; Body Actions	6, 7
Follow-the-String Golf (7)	Hitting a Ball	2
Freeze (10)	All Locomotor Skills	1
Freeze Balance Tag (3)	Static Balancing	3

Games	Performance Objective	Book
Funny Clown (6)	All Rhythmic Skills	5
Gallop Tag (4)	Galloping, Hopping, Jumping, Running, Skipping	1
Gathering Objects (5)	Parachute	3
Giants and Dragons (7)	Running, Skipping, Jumping, Galloping, Sliding, Bicycle Riding	1, 7
Giants and Dwarfs (9)	Trunk and Leg Flexibility	4
Happy Story (9)	Expressive Communication	5
Head, Shoulders, Knees, and Toes (7)	Expressive Communication, Singing Games	5
Hill Dill (9)	Galloping, Hopping, Jumping, Running, Skipping, Sliding	1
Hit the Beat (9)	Move to Even Beat, Accent	5
Hokey Pokey	Body Parts	6
Hoop, Hop, Jump (7)	Hopping, Jumping	1
Hopscotch (9)	Static Balancing	3
Hopscotch, modified (9)	Hopping, Jumping	1
Hot Potato (9)	Rolling, Throwing, Catching, Bouncing, Kicking a Ball	2
Hot Rods (9)	Galloping, Hopping, Jumping, Running, Skipping, Sliding	1
How High Can You Fly? (8)	Swing on Swing	7
I Am a Balloon (10)	Rest and Relaxation	4
Ice Cream Cone Game (7)	Dynamic Balancing	3
If You're Happy (7)	Expressive Communication, Singing Games	5
I'm a Little Teapot (7)	Expressive Communication, Singing Games	5
Indian Walk Through Woods (7)	Galloping, Hopping, Jumping, Running, Skipping, Sliding	1
Isn't It Fun? (9)	Expressive Communication	5
I Went to School One Morning (7)	Expressive Communication, Singing Games	5
Jack-in-the-Box (7)	Expressive Communication, Singing Games	5

GAMES	PERFORMANCE OBJECTIVE	BOOK
Jello Jiggle (10)	Rest and Relaxation	4
Jet Pilots (9)	All Locomotor Skills	1
Jumping Races (7)	Jumping, Running, Skipping	1
Jumping Rope (7)	Jumping	1
Jump In and Out of Tires (7)	Jumping	1
Jump Rabbit Jump (7)	Hopping, Jumping	1
Jump the Shot (7)	Hopping, Jumping	1
Jungle Gym Tag (9)	Climbing Stairs	1
Keep It Up (9)	Rolling and Kicking a Ball	2
Kick the Can (9)	Kicking a Ball	2
Kick to the Target (9)	Kicking a Ball	2
Ladder Game (8)	Dynamic Balancing	3
Leader Class (9)	Throwing and Catching a Ball	2
Let's Pretend (9)	All Body Movement Skills	6
Let's Relax (9)	Rest and Relaxation	4
Let's Walk Around the Circle (7)	Expressive Communication, Singing Games	5
Lift a Box (9)	Lift and Carry Objects	4
Lift and Carry (9)	Lift and Carry Objects	4
Lifting Relay (9)	Lift and Carry Objects	4
Line Carry (9)	Lift and Carry Objects	4
Little Rabbit (7)	Expressive Communcation, Singing Games	5
London Bridge (1)	Move to Uneven Beat, Expressive Communication, Singing Games	5
Magic Ball (7)	Lift and Carry Objects	4
Making Shapes (9)	Shapes and Sizes	6
Mary Had a Little Lamb (4)	Move to Even Beat, Expressive Communication, Singing Games	5

GAMES	PERFORMANCE OBJECTIVE	BOOK
Medicine Ball (7)	Lift and Carry Objects	4
Mirror Man (3)	Body Actions, Body Parts	6
Modified Shuffleboard (7)	Hang from a Bar	7
Modified Soccer (7)	Kicking a Ball	2
Modified Tetherball (7)	Hitting a Ball	2
Monkey Bar Hang Relay (6)	Hang from a Bar	7
Monkey in the Middle (1)	Catching a Ball	2
Monkey See, Monkey Do (7)	Expressive Communication, Singing Games	5
Moving Games (9)	Lift and Carry Objects	4
Moving Playground (9)	Body Actions	6
Mulberry Bush (4)	Move to Even Beat, Expressive Communication	5
My Airplane (7)	Expressive Communication	5
My Little Puppy (6)	All Rhythmic Skills	5
My Very Own Space (9)	Personal Space	6
Name Change (9)	Parachute	3
Net Ball (9)	Throwing a Ball	2
Obstacle Course (3)	All Play Skills	7
One, Two, Buckle My Shoe (3)	Move to Uneven Beat	5
On and Off the Blanket (7)	Hopping, Jumping	1
Open, Shut Them (7)	Expressive Communication, Singing Games	5
Paper Ball Play (9)	Throwing a Ball	2
Parachute Golf (5)	Parachute	3
Partner Hop (7)	Hopping, Jumping	1
Pat-a-Cake (7)	Expressive Communication, Singing Games	5
Poison (9)	Galloping, Hopping, Jumping, Running, Skipping, Sliding	1

GAMES	PERFORMANCE OBJECTIVE	BOOK
Popcorn (3)	Parachute	3
Pop Goes the Weasel (5)	Jumping	1
Potpourri (5)	Parachute	3
Push Ball Relay (9)	Hitting a Ball	2
Push Broom (7)	Push and Pull Object	7
Pushing a Box as a Group (7)	Push and Pull Object	7
Putt It (7)	Hitting a Ball	2
Raggedy Ann and Andy (10)	Rest and Relaxation	4
Red and Blue City (6)	Hitting a Ball	2
Rig-a-Jig-Jig (7)	Galloping, Hopping, Jumping, Running, Skipping, Sliding	1
Right and Left (9)	All Body Movement Skills	6
Roll Away (7)	Dynamic and Static Balancing; Log, Forward, and Backward Rolls	3
Rolling Down the Tubes (7)	Running	1
Roll and Toss (7)	Forward Roll	3
Rolling Down Grassy Hills (7)	Log, Forward, and Backward Rolls	3
Rolling in the Snow (Angels in Snow) (7)	Log, Forward, and Backward Rolls	3
Rolling Into and Out of Blanket (7)	Log, Forward, and Backward Rolls	3
Rolling Races (8)	Log, Forward, and Backward Rolls	3
Roll Like a Ball (7)	Forward Roll	3
Round the Sun (9)	Galloping, Hopping, Jumping, Running, Skipping, Sliding	1
Run and Roll (9)	Forward Roll	3
Sandbox Relay (7)	Push and Pull Object	7
Scat (9)	Body Parts	7
Scatter Play (9)	Lift and Carry Objects	4

GAMES	PERFORMANCE OBJECTIVE	BOOK
Scoop Catch (7)	Throwing and Catching a Ball	2
Scooterboard Races (9)	Travel on Scooterboard	7
Scooter Kickball (7)	Kicking a Ball	2
See My Fingers (7)	Expressive Communication, Singing Games Walking, Walking	5
Shot Gun (9)	Throwing, Catching, and Bouncing a Ball	2
Shuttle Run Relay (9)	Trunk and Leg Flexibility	4
Simon Says (3)	All Play Skills	7
Skip Around the Block (9)	Skipping	1
Skipping Hill Dill (9)	Skipping	1
Skipping Poison (9)	Galloping, Hopping, Jumping, Running, Skipping, Sliding	1
Skipping Relay (9)	Galloping, Hopping, Jumping, Running, Skipping, Sliding	1
Sliding into Pool (7)	Sliding	1
Snake Tag (5)	Parachute	3
Space Walk (9)	General Space	6
Static Balance (9)	Static Balancing	3
Statues in the Garden (9)	Static Balancing	3
Stretch the Rope (9)	Personal Space	6
Stride Ball (8)	All Ball-Handling Skills	2
Stop and Go (7)	Jumping	1
Suspended Ball (7)	Hitting a Ball	2
Tall and Small (9)	Directions in Space	6
Target Bowling (9)	Rolling a Ball	2
Target Practice (9)	Throwing a Ball	2
Ten Little Indians (4)	Move to Even Beat, Expressive Communication, Singing Games	5
Ten Little Jingle Bells (6)	All Rhythmic Skills	5

GAMES	PERFORMANCE OBJECTIVE	BOOK
The Chase (5)	Parachute	3
The Farmer in the Dell (6)	Move to Even Beat, Expressive Communication, Singing Games	5
This Old Man (7)	Expressive Communication, Singing Games	5
Thousand-legged Worm (7)	Galloping, Hopping, Jumping, Running, Skipping, Sliding	1
Throw (Kick), Rebound, Catch (7)	Throwing, Catching, and Kicking a Ball	2
Toss-Jump-Pick (7)	Jumping	1
Trunk-Leg Relay (9)	Trunk and Leg Flexibility	4
Trunk Lifts (9)	Situps	4
Tug of War (7)	Hang from a Bar	7
Twinkle, Twinkle, Little Star (4)	Move to Even Beat, Singing Games	5
Twister (5)	Static Balancing	3
Two Little Blackbirds (7)	Expressive Communication, Singing Games	5
Train Station (7)	Galloping, Hopping, Jumping, Running, Skipping, Sliding	1
Upstairs, Downstairs (9)	Climbing Stairs	1
Walk-Run Relay (9)	Walk-Run for Endurance	4
Water Play with Buckets (7)	Lift and Carry Objects	4
Water Slide (7)	Sliding	1
Where Are You? (9)	All Body Movement Skills	6
Where Is Thumbkin? (7)	Expressive Communication, Singing Games	5
Wiggle Like a Snake (7)	Expressive Communication	5
Yankee Doodle (4)	Move to Even Beat, Expressive Communication, Singing Games	5
Zoo Song (7)	Expressive Communication, Singing Games	5
ZZZZ (10)	Rest and Relaxation	4

Game Sources

1. Block, Susan D. *Me and I'm Great: Physical Education for Children Three through Eight*. Minnesota: Burgess, 1977.

2. Cherry, Clare. *Creative Movement for the Developing Child*. California: David S. Lake/Fearon, 1971.

3. Curtis, Sandra R. *The Joy of Movement in Early Childhood*. New York: Teachers College Press, 1982.

4. Dauer, Victor. *Essential Movement Experiences for Preschool and Primary Children*. Minnesota: Burgess, 1972.

5. French, R., and M. Horvat. *Parachute Movement Activities*. California: Front Row Experiences, 1983.

6. Gallahue, David. *Developmental Movement Experiences for Children*. New York: John Wiley, 1982.

7. Littman, Karen, and Lin Leslie. *Preschool Recreation Enrichment Program Project (PREP): Motor and Associated Learning, Preschool Program for Handicapped Children*. Washington, DC: Research and Demonstration Project, U.S. Department of Education, Bureau of Education for Handicapped, 1976.

8. Wessel, Janet, et al. *I CAN Preprimary Motor and Play Skills*. Michigan: Instructional Media Center, Michigan State University, 1980.

9. ———. *I CAN Primary Skills Physical Education Curriculum*. Illinois: Hubbard, 1976.

10. Torbet, Marianne. *Follow Me—A Handbook of Movement Activities for Children*. New Jersey: Prentice Hall, 1980.

APPENDIX E:
A TOY GUIDE FOR CHILDREN WITH SPECIAL NEEDS

Toys are early educational tools. This guide lists a variety of toys that stimulate various developmental functions in children with special needs. It is not an exhaustive list, but it demonstrates the types of toys available in stores nationwide and gives examples of their functions.

The toys listed here are coded according to the function they may help to develop.

Function	Code
Auditory	A
Balance and Coordination	B/C
Educational	E
Eye-Hand Coordination	E/H
Imaginative Problem Solving	I/P
Tactile (touching, feeling)	T
Visual	V

The toys listed here are also grouped according to the age at which they would most probably be introduced to other children: toddlers, or preschool and early elementary school. The toys may be appropriate for more than one age level or function, however.

A list of adaptive equipment specially designed to enable children with various physical disabilities to play with toys and develop skills is also provided.

TODDLERS

A, E, E/H, V   **Angel Bunny Take Along Activity Toy**
Attaches to stroller or car seat. Soft book with activities inside.
Mattel. Toy-R-Us

E/H, V   **Balls in Bowl**
Balls, with objects inside, may be tossed into the bowl.
Johnson & Johnson. Service Merchandise

E/H, T   **Bath Activity Center**
Attaches to tub; water play.
Fisher Price. Toys-R-Us

E/H, T   **Bathtime Water Works**
Toys for water play, stacking. Container floats while child plays.
Johnson & Johnson. Toys-R-Us

A   **Big Bird Talking Telephone**
Push buttons and Sesame Street characters talk to you.
Hasbro. Service Merchandise

B/C　　　　　**Big Bounce**
　　　　　　　　36" inflatable trampoline
　　　　　　　　G. Pierce Toy Manufacturing Co., Inc. Service Merchandise

A, V　　　　　**Big Mouth Singers**
　　　　　　　　8 characters sing out notes as piano keys are pushed.
　　　　　　　　Child Guidance. Toys-R-Us

E, E/H　　　　**Big Shape and Sort Cube**
　　　　　　　　3 shapes to sort on each side of cube. Top of cube opens; child can store shapes inside.
　　　　　　　　Chicco. Toys-R-Us

I/P　　　　　**Big Tool Bench**
　　　　　　　　Bench with large plastic tools.
　　　　　　　　Playskool. Toys-R-Us

B/C, I/P　　　**Bubblemower**
　　　　　　　　Push lawn mower that blows soap bubbles.
　　　　　　　　Playskool. Toys-R-Us

E　　　　　　**Candyland**
　　　　　　　　Child draws the colored cards and moves to corresponding square on board. Great first
　　　　　　　　board game.
　　　　　　　　Milton Bradley. Toys-R-Us

E　　　　　　**Candyland Bingo**
　　　　　　　　Bingo done by rows of colors.
　　　　　　　　Milton Bradley. Toys-R-Us

A, V　　　　　**Chicken 'n Egg Poppin Top**
　　　　　　　　Chicken and egg inside spinning top.
　　　　　　　　Ohio Art. Toys-R-Us

I/P　　　　　**Child-size Broom**
　　　　　　　　Toys-R-Us

I/P　　　　　**Child-size Dustmop**
　　　　　　　　Toys-R-Us

T, V　　　　　**Chubbles**
　　　　　　　　Eyes light up. Some are activated by light, others by sound.
　　　　　　　　Animal Fair. Toys-R-Us

E/H　　　　　**Cobbler's Bench**
　　　　　　　　Pegs to pound into bench, all wood.
　　　　　　　　Playskool. Toys-R-Us

E/H　　　　　**Colored Wood Blocks**
　　　　　　　　49 pieces, brightly colored wood blocks.
　　　　　　　　Playskool. Toys-R-Us

B/C　　　　　**Corn Popper**
　　　　　　　　Push toy. Colorful balls pop as child walks and pushes toy.
　　　　　　　　Fisher Price. Service Merchandise

A, V　　　　　**Crib and Playpen Chime Ball**
　　　　　　　　Heavyweight ball. Colorful scene inside. Chimes as it rolls.
　　　　　　　　Fisher Price. Service Merchandise

I/P, E, E/H	**Discovery Cottage** A cottage that is an activity center. Fisher Price. Service Merchandise
A, E, E/H	**Disney's Gummi Bear** Bounces like a ball. It is really a soft creature with ball attached. Fisher Price. Toys-R-Us
E/H	**Duplo Baby Rocking Horse** Horse, man, and rocker that fit together. Lego. Toys-R-Us
E/H	**Duplo Pre-School Sets** Building sets with only a few pieces. Lego. Toys-R-Us
A, E, E/H	**8 in 1 Play Center** Hexagon-shaped toys pull out from frame. Each is a different activity. Carry handle. Shellcore. Toys-R-Us
T, V	**Globug and Globutterfly** Activated by being held tight. Soft. Hasbro. Circus World.
A, V	**Gloworm Musical Jack-in-the-Box** Gloworm pops out of the box. Playskool. Toys-R-Us
A, T	**Grab a Ball** Indentations make ball easy to hold. Squeaks. Chicco. Toys-R-Us
B/C, E/H, I/P	**Great Big Blocks** Large plastic blocks of different shapes. Little Tikes. Toys-R-Us
A, V	**Hamster** Electronic. You clap and it comes. Axlon. Toys-R-Us
I/P	**Magic Vac** Vacuum that lights up and makes sound. (No batteries.) Fisher Price. Toys-R-Us
A, I/P	**Marching Band** Drum holds other instruments. All plastic. Fisher Price. Toys-R-Us
I/P	**Medical Kit** Great for pretend. Fisher Price. Toys-R-Us
A	**Mickey Mouse Talking Telephone** Push buttons, and Disney characters talk to you. Hasbro. Service Merchandise
T, V, A	**Musical Gloworm** It glows when activated by light. Hasbro. Circus World

B/C	**Nerf Football** Parker Brothers. Toys-R-Us
E, E/H	**Pick-up and Peek Wood Puzzle** Puzzle with knobs for easier handling. Various numbers of pieces. Fisher Price. Toys-R-Us
I/P, T	**Playdough** 4-pack. Kenner. Service Merchandise
I/P, E/H	**Power Workshop** Plastic drill, bench, and caddy. Fisher Price. Service Merchandise
A, E/H, E	**Rhythm Rollers** Truck with cylinders that stack and rattle. Johnson & Johnson. Toys-R-Us
E, E/H	**Rock a Stack** Rings of varied sizes to stack. Fisher Price. Toys-R-Us
A, E	**See 'N Say** Fun with Sounds. Zoo. Bee Says (alphabet sounds). Fisher Price. Toys-R-Us
E, E/H	**Shape Sorter Transporter** Shape sorter and truck. Johnson & Johnson. Service Merchandise
I/P	**Sink Set** Press sink faucet and water comes out; includes dishes. Fisher Price. Toys-R-Us
B/C	**Sit 'n Spin** Child sits on disk and spins self around. Kenner. Toys-R-Us
E/H, T, A	**Six Soft Squeak Blocks** Textured and easy to hold. Chicco. Toys-R-Us
I/P	**Smocks** Plastic, with pockets. Fisher Price. Toys-R-Us
E/H	**Snap Lock Animals** Animal-shaped beads that snap together. Fisher Price. Toys-R-Us
E, E/H	**Stack and Dump Truck** Truck with post and rings for stacking. Rings can also be lined up and carried on truck. Johnson & Johnson. Toys-R-Us
E, E/H	**Stack 'n Store Nesting Cubes** Cubes that stack and nest. Little Tikes. Toys-R-Us

E, E/H   **Stacking Cubes**
                    Smaller cubes to stack and nest.
                    Playskool. Toys-R-Us

A   **Talking Big Bird**
                    Talks when child pulls string.
                    Playskool. Toys-R-Us

A, E/H   **Tap a Tune Piano**
                    Colored keys, easy to push; carry handle.
                    Little Tikes. Toys-R-Us

I/P   **Tea Set and Tray**
                    Plastic set.
                    Fisher Price. Toys-R-Us

E, E/H   **10-Piece Baby Blocks**
                    Indented toward center for easy gripping.
                    Playskool. Toys-R-Us

E, E/H   **30 Colored Wood Beads and Stringer**
                    Beads of various shapes and colors to string.
                    Connor Preschool. Toys-R-Us

A, V   **Toot a Loo Loco**
                    Child can watch gears as they move.
                    Child Guidance. Service Merchandise

E/H, T   **Tub Fun**
                    Soft activity center for tub.
                    Fisher Price. Toys-R-Us

I/P   **Tuff Stuff Shopping Basket**
                    Mattel. Toys-R-Us

I/P   **Tuff Stuff Wheelbarrow**
                    Mattel. Toys-R-Us

A, E, E/H   **Turn and Learn Activity Center**
                    Activity box on swivel base.
                    Fisher Price. Service Merchandise

E, V   **Tutor Typer**
                    When child depresses easy-touch keys, letters with associated pictures appear.
                    Tomy. Toys-R-Us

A, E/H   **Xylophone**
                    Instrument and pull toy.
                    Fisher Price. Service Merchandise

A, E/H   **Xylo Drum**
                    Small xylophone on one side, drum on other.
                    Fisher Price. Toys-R-Us

A, E, V   **Alphie II**
Child's first computer. Matching, music, math, spelling, musical chairs, color memory.
Playskool. Toys-R-Us

A, E, V   **Alphie II Additional Learning Sets**
Playskool. Toys-R-Us

E/H, I/P   **Basic Building Set**
Lego's plastic blocks.
Lego. Toys-R-Us

E/H, I/P   **Bristle Blocks**
Put together easily, though they require some strength to pull apart.
Playskool. Toys-R-Us

A   **Crazy Combo**
Connect the pieces to make a variety of instruments.
Fisher Price. Toys-R-Us

E/H, V   **Etch a Sketch**
Turns knobs and draw sketchlike pictures.
Ohio Art. Toys-R-Us

E, T, E/H   **Hi Ho Cherry O**
Take cherries out of tree and put into buckets. The tree has depressions to hold cherries
in place.
Golden. Toys-R-Us

I/P   **Kitchen Set**
Dishes and tabletop burner for pretend.
Fisher Price. Toys-R-Us

E, B/C   **Letter Woodblock Wagon**
24 wood blocks with alphabet printed on them. Also a pull toy.
Playskool. Service Merchandise

E, V   **Light 'n Learn**
Find correct choice and it lights up.
Milton Bradley. Service Merchandise

I/P, E/H   **Lincoln Logs—Original**
Child can create log dwellings.
Playskool. Toys-R-Us

E/H, V   **Lite-Brite**
Create colorful pictures that light up. Peg and picture refills available.
Hasbro. Toys-R-Us

E, V   **Magnetic Alphabet Board**
Set up vertically.
Sand. Service Merchandise

E, V   **Memory**
Card-matching memory game. Varieties: Original, Animal Families, Fronts and Backs.
Milton Bradley. Toys-R-Us

A   **Mickey Talking Toothbrush**
Mickey Mouse talks to you while you brush.
Lakeside. Service Merchandise

E/H   **Mr. Potato Head Family**
Child assembles faces and costumes.
Hasbro Preschool Service Merchandise

I/P   **Phone Friends**
Play phones that work like walkie-talkies.
Fisher Price. Toys-R-Us

E, E/H   **Play Desk**
Letter and number skills. Portable.
Fisher Price. Toys-R-Us

T, I/P   **Playdough (3-lb bucket)**
Kenner. Toys-R-Us

T, I/P   **Playdough Rainbow Pack (8 colors)**
Kenner. Toys-R-Us

A, I/P   **Power Workshop**
Drill and bits.
Fisher Price. Toys-R-Us

E/H   **Sewing Cards**
Picture cards with holes to lace. Fine motor skill work.
Colorforms. Toys-R-Us

V   **Spirotot**
Device that helps child draw colored pencil designs.
Kenner. Toys-R-Us

V   **Swirl Art**
Squeeze colors onto turntable and make thousands of different designs.
Nasta. Service Merchandise

A, E   **Tape Recorder**
Heavyweight plastic.
Fisher Price. Toys-R-Us

E/H, V   **Toybars**
Standing frame to hang toys from—includes 2 toys and 9 toy clips.
Century. Toys-R-Us

E/H, V   **Tracking Tube**
Rattle with red floating ball that moves as rattle is turned. Soft ends.
Johnson & Johnson. Toys-R-Us

A, E, V   **Teddy Ruxpin**
Animated bear. Talks along with cassettes. (Additional book and cassette sets available.)
World of Wonder. Toys-R-Us

E/H, B/C	**Topple**
	Game—stacking and balancing.
	Pressman. Toys-R-Us

E/H	**Trouble**
	Move colored pegs around path. Counting game.
	Milton Bradley. Toys-R-Us

B/C	**Twister**
	Spin dial and put hands and feet on large dots of same color.
	Milton Bradley. Service Merchandise

E/H, B/C	**Waffle Blocks**
	Large, colorful blocks that look like waffles.
	Little Tikes. Service Merchandise

ADAPTIVE EQUIPMENT FOR CHILDREN WITH SPECIAL NEEDS

Addresses and phone numbers of suppliers follow the list of equipment.

E/H	**Adjustable Batting Tee**
	Height adjusts from 27" to 41". 1-P2915.
	Kaplan School Supply

B/C	**Aluminum Swing Chair Seat**
	Heavy-duty cast aluminum. 13 $^1/_4$" wide x 5 $^1/_4$" deep x 9 $^1/_2$" high. 1-P3424 DS.
	Kaplan School Supply

B/C	**Balance Board Set**
	Adjustable balancing set. 4" wide, 5" off ground. 4 boards, each 44" long x 4" wide. 1-P10919 DS.
	Kaplan School Supply

B/C	**Balance Disc**
	Balance skills on functional platform. Safety treads eliminate slipping; protective guard rails; 27° tilt maximum. 1-P7800.
	Kaplan School Supply

E/H	**Bean Bag Alphabet**
	Upper and lower cases. 53B5A.
	Kaplan School Supply

E/H	**Bean Bag Numbers**
	1–10. 53B5N.
	Kaplan School Supply

E/H	**Bean Bag Toss Game**
	Durable cardboard with wood frame and stand. Measures 18" x 23". Comes with three beanbags. 1-P3619.
	Kaplan School Supply

E/H	**Classroom Bowling Set**
	10 pins—plastic, 12" tall—and two balls. P-7615.
	Playhouse

E/H	**Color Bean Bags** Set of 8. 53B5-C. Things from Bell
E/H	**Foam Ball** Basketball. 1-P3658. Small (4"). 1-P1901. Large (7"—soccer ball, volleyball, kickball). 1-P1903. Playhouse
E/H	**Foam Bowling Pins** 12" high x 4" diameter. Each pin weighs $3\frac{1}{2}$ oz. Set of 10. P–761. Playhouse
E/H	**Geometric Shapes** Foam disks with 4 shapes (circle, square, triangle, rectangle). 5 S709S. Things from Bell.
B/C	**Incline Mat** For forward and backward rolls. 36" x 72" x 16". 1-P3753 DS. 60" x 84" x 18". 1-P2538 DS. Kaplan School Supply
B/C	**Inflatable Cage Ball** Develop balance skills and increase flexibility by lying across ball on one's back or front. 18". 1-P2345 DS. 30". 1-P2347 DS. Kaplan School Supply
B/C	**Jumping Tube** Inflates to 4 feet. Can be used as trampoline or water raft. 1-P0200. Kaplan School Supply
B/C	**Jump Ropes** Flexible, colored, $5/16$" rope with wood handles. $6\frac{1}{2}$ foot. 2JR6 (one). 5JR6D (a dozen). 16 foot. 2JR16 (one). 5JR16D (a dozen). Things from Bell
E/H	**Learning Fleece Balls** 4" balls. Set of 8 with red, blue, green, and yellow. 4235. Things from Bell
B/C, E/H	**Mobile Mats** Designed to strengthen neck and back muscles and encourage reciprocal motion in upper extremities. Padded platform, 16" x 43", with 2 velcro straps to secure student to mat. 1–P8590 DS. Kaplan School Supply

E/H　　　　　**Multicolor Pushball**
　　　　　　　　18" diameter. P-1253.
　　　　　　　　30" diameter. P-9378.
　　　　　　　　48" diameter. P-4448.
　　　　　　　　72" diameter. P-9419.
　　　　　　　　Flaghouse

E/H　　　　　**Plastic Bat and Ball**
　　　　　　　　30" bat and a ball. 1-P3619.
　　　　　　　　Kaplan School Supply

E/H　　　　　**Play Canopy**
　　　　　　　　Multicolor nylon parachute.
　　　　　　　　6-foot diameter. 1-P011 DS.
　　　　　　　　12-foot diameter. 1-P2743 DS.
　　　　　　　　24-foot diameter. 1-P3381 DS.
　　　　　　　　Kaplan School Supply

E/H　　　　　**Playground Balls**
　　　　　　　　7". P1907.
　　　　　　　　8 $1/2$". 1P2093.
　　　　　　　　10". 1P1904.
　　　　　　　　13". 1P2519.
　　　　　　　　Kaplan School Supply

B/C, Eye/Foot　　**Poly Balance Beam**
　　　　　　　　Balance beam sits on floor. Rubberized vinyl. 4" wide x $1^1/_2$" thick. Folds and comes
　　　　　　　　with carrying case. PE-10.
　　　　　　　　Opportunities for Learning

B/C, E/H　　　**Poly Pads**
　　　　　　　　For coordination, locomotion, left-right recognition. Nontoxic, rubberized red vinyl. Each
　　　　　　　　set has 12 poly pads.
　　　　　　　　Large handprints (6" x 9 $1/2$"). PE-111.
　　　　　　　　Large footprints (4 $1/2$" x 9 $1/2$"). PE-211.
　　　　　　　　Directional arrows (6" x 9 $1/2$"). PE-301.
　　　　　　　　Hop spots (10" diameter). PE-501.
　　　　　　　　Opportunities for Learning

T, E/H　　　　**Portable Sand Box**
　　　　　　　　Sandbox with cover. 32" x 24", 8" deep. 1-P12082.
　　　　　　　　Kaplan School Supply

E/H　　　　　**Preschool Bat and Ball Set**
　　　　　　　　Plastic. 18" ball with baseball bat.
　　　　　　　　Bat and ball. P-5825.
　　　　　　　　Jumbo bat and ball. P-5826.
　　　　　　　　Flaghouse

B/C　　　　　**Preschool Climber**
　　　　　　　　Child-sealed chain net, staggered bilateral ladder for climbing.
　　　　　　　　4' 6" high with 12" ladder (100 lbs, portable). 2302-131.
　　　　　　　　Things from Bell

B/C   **Rainbow Tumbling Mat**
6' x 4', lightweight, foldable mats of same size can connect together. 1P10904.
Kaplan School Supply

B/C   **Red Wagon**
Tip resistant. Steel handrails and handle that can't swing up (46 lbs). Ages 2–8.
1P9867 DS.
Kaplan School Supply

I/P   **Ride 'Em Car**
Good for large muscle activity, imagination, and dramatic play. 1P346 DS.
Kaplan School Supply

E   **Safety Cone**
12" fluorescent orange PVC vinyl; nontip base. Great as relay, goal, or obstacle marker.
1-P5935.
Kaplan School Supply

E/H   **Saftee Hockey**
7" foam ball, 4" puck, set of 10 sticks. P1790.
Flaghouse

B/C   **Scooter Board**
Each side has safety grip and double-ballbearing swivel caster (12" x 12" x 1 $^1/_2$").
1-P5935.
Set of 6 scooterboards with stacking pole. 1-P4901.
Kaplan School Supply

E/H, I/P, B/C   **Snapwalls**
30" square x 2" thick panels for play structures. Set of 10 walls in colors (65 lbs).
P-4268.
Flaghouse

E/H, B/C   **Trikes**
Built-in safety features: low center of gravity, heavier weight to prevent tipping, solid disk
wheels to protect hands and feet.
3–4 years (12" wheels, 27 lbs). 1-P0870 DS.
4–8 years (14" wheels, 30 lbs). 1-P3204 DS.
Kaplan School Supply

B/C   **VCS Foam Steps**
Fun for climbing, soft enough to absorb falls. Vinyl and foam filler. 33" x 24" x 21" (20
lbs). 105-02.
VCS, Inc.

B/C   **Wheelbarrow**
Ground grip. 1-P3424.
Kaplan School Supply

SUPPLIERS OF ADAPTIVE EQUIPMENT

Flaghouse
150 N. MacQuesten Pkwy.
Mt. Vernon, NY 10550
1-800-221-5185

Kaplan School Supply
600 Jonestown Road
Winston-Salem, NC 27103
1-800-334-2014

Opportunities for Learning
20417 Nordoff St., Dept. EB
Chatsworth, CA 91311
1-800-341-2535

Things from Bell
4 Lincoln Ave.
P.O. Box 706
Cortland, NY 13045
607-753-8291

VCS, Inc.
155 State St.
Hackensack, NJ 07601
1-800-526-4856

A catalogue of specially designed electronic controls for toys, switches, computer aids, and communications devices for special-needs children is available from

Steven Kanor, Ph.D, Inc.
Toys for Special Children
c/o Michael Garb
4068 Bayberry Lane
Seaford, NY 11783